**Berlitz**®

# Madrid

Front cover: Café life on Plaza Mayor

Right: Guards at the Royal Palace

**Plaza Mayor.** Take a seat at a terrace café and watch the world go by at the busy centre of local social life. See page 28.

**Museo Nacional Centro de Arte Reina Sofía.** A popular showcase of art of the 20th and 21st centuries, including work by Picasso and Luis Buñuel. See page 50.

**Puerta del Sol.** The plaza's clock tower overlooks the bustling heart of Madrid and chimes in Spain's New Year revelry. See page 36.

**El Escorial.** The palace created by Felipe II, where Spain's Golden Age is writ large. See page 70.

**The Prado.** Spain's rich artistic heritage is conserved in one of the world's most prestigious museums. See page 42.

**Monasterio de las Descalzas Reales.** A unique chance to see the artistic heritage of a working convent over 450 years. See page 36.

**Plaza Santa Ana.** A great place to start *el tapeo*, the 'tapas crawl'. See page 38.

**Palacio Real.** Elegant centre of royal Madrid. See page 32.

**La Ermita de San Antonio de la Florida.** Goya's frescoes adorn the cupola of this 18th century chapel. See page 68.

**Parque del Buen Retiro.** Its trees, lawns and lake make this Madrid's most child-friendly green space. See page 52.

# A PERFECT DAY

**9.00am** **Santa Ana**

Join locals for coffee and fried *churros* as the day gets underway on this classic tree-lined *plaza* in the city's 18th-century quarter. Don't miss the colourful tiled friezes on bars around the square.

**1.00pm** **Art and *aperitivos***

Take a break in the top floor café of Herzog de Meuron's CaixaForum arts centre where you can sip an *aperitivo* and look down on the adjacent vertical garden, a rich tapestry of globally sourced plant varieties.

**11.00am** **The Prado**

Visit one of the world's greatest art galleries. Do not miss the newly restored Renaissance Patio de los Jerónimos. The Spanish paintings, largely collected by the royal family, include masterworks by Diego Velázquez and Francisco de Goya.

**10.00am** **Green oasis**

Explore the beautifully tended Real Jardín Botánico where dahlias were first planted in Europe. Three greenhouses are filled with desert and tropical flora and there is an appealing garden gift shop.

**2.00pm** **Classic *cocido***

Madrid's celebrated chickpea stew, or *cocido*, with its own soup and vegetables, is cooked the old-fashioned way in earthenware pots over charcoal at La Bola, where you lunch with locals at a leisurely pace.

# IN MADRID

**5.30pm** | **Shop till you drop**

Pedestrianised Calle de Fuencarral, running off Gran Vía, is the city's most fashionable shopping drag. Here you can find hip Spanish fashion brands from Camper shoes to Custo and Hoss Intropia clothes, plus other European fashion. Cafés, bars and ice cream parlours offer retreats from the street.

**10.30pm** | **Flamenco**

Book ahead for the late show at one of the city's *tablaos*, or flamenco clubs, like Casa Patas. Here you will witness an authentic flamenco experience and see artists perform flamenco song, guitar and dance in an intimate and atmospheric environment.

**7.30pm** | **Tapas time**

Enjoy the city's magical dusk light with a *paseo*, or evening stroll, through the sloping old streets that link the Plaza Mayor to the Cava Baja in the medieval old town. Locals end the day there with a glass of fine wine and tapas in coaching inns and designer bars.

**4.00pm** | *Guernica*

Pablo Picasso conceived *Guernica*, one of the 20th century's greatest paintings, as a protest against the Nazi bombing of the Basque village, in 1937. See it hanging alongside his preparatory drawings on the second floor of the Museo Nacional Centro de Arte Reina Sofia.

**9.00pm** | **Dinner date**

Move on for dinner at Casa Lucio, a classic Madrid restaurant on Cava Baja that offers genuine Castilian cuisine for every pocket. Choose between wood-roast meats, 'broken eggs' or baked fish.

# CONTENTS

Features

# INTRODUCTION

Madrid was little more than a farming town on the arid central plains of Castile when Felipe II plucked it from his royal cap in 1561 and proclaimed it home to the Spanish Court. Ever since then man-made Madrid, which took the reins of Spain's Golden Age, hasn't stopped growing and asserting itself. Though one of Europe's youngest capitals, it's had time and the ambition to rival Spain's more historic cities, including Seville and Valencia. Today it is Spain's political and economic hub. Only Barcelona matches its metropolitan importance.

## The Heart of Spain

Behind Felipe II's royal decree lay a clear logic: Madrid, smack in the centre of Iberia, would promote the monarchy's authority over regional power bases in a newly unified Spain. Today, Madrid is that cohesive centre and more. It is a city to which people have migrated from all over Spain in search of new opportunities; a place where few people claim deep roots.

Yet at the centre of the modern metropolis, a region of just over 6 million people, its medieval heart lies almost untouched, the alleyways silent at night. For while Spain has leaped forward economically since the 1970s, Madrid is no less characteristically Iberian for that and revels in its traditional way of life. Once, its immigrants were from the Spanish

### One step to heaven

'De Madrid al cielo' is a popular saying, which means 'From Madrid, one step to heaven.' As western Europe's highest capital, Madrid boasts spectacular sierra skies and autumn sunsets, captured by Velázquez in his paintings.

Typical Madrid facades

countryside. Today, its newcomers more often come from Latin America and Eastern Europe, but their new customs and fiestas are equally absorbed into the local pattern of life.

Other regions of Spain, such as Catalonia and the Basque country, are more proudly independent in their traditions. Barcelona, Granada and older Castilian court cities possess greater architecture. Many smaller Spanish cities have finer historic quarters. But Madrileños don't begrudge those places anything. Their city may be a planned bureaucrat's town, like Brasilia or Washington, but its buzzing quality of life, keeps Madrid just one rung down from heaven, or so the local saying goes – and many Madrileños believe it.

## La Noche: Madrid's Nightlife

Gregarious at heart, Madrileños are night creatures, hopping in and out of *tabernas* (cave-like taverns), restaurants and bars for tapas, Spanish wine and animated conversation until the early hours. The *movida* of the early 1980s, a spontaneous burst of creative nightlife, has given Madrid a name it works hard to maintain. Nightlife still starts and goes on late–very late– with after-hours clubs and bar-hoppers. A lack of sleep can always be remedied later, a Madrileño might tell you, as he or she tops off a late night with early-morning *chocolate con churros* (sticks of fried dough dipped into strong, thick hot chocolate) before heading home in the dawn hours.

## Culture Capital

In recent years the city has nurtured Spain's most sophisti-cated cultural life: opera, theatre, *zarzuela* (a form of light comic opera), contemporary dance, jazz and rock, film, circus and graffiti. All have found new audiences here, as has fla-menco, Spain's most unique art form.

But Madrid's single greatest cultural draw, remains its clus-ter of superb art museums. On the grand Paseo del Prado

Busy Plaza de Cibeles

are three of Europe's finest: the world-class Museo Nacional del Prado, the Museo Thyssen-Bornemisza and the Museo Nacional Centro de Arte Reina Sofía, currently home to Pablo Picasso's monumental painting, *Guernica*. Madrid's collection of Spanish Old Masters – Velázquez, El Greco, Goya, Zurbarán and more – is unrivalled.

## Geography

In terms of scale, Madrid's city centre hardly feels like that of a capital city – anyone from London, New York or even Paris is bound to have this impression – and it is easily covered on foot. The city's heart is Old (or Habsburg) Madrid, a largely 16th-century city built around the narrow, winding streets of the earlier Muslim settlement. Its centrepiece is the splendid porticoed Plaza Mayor, rebuilt three times after fires. Nearby are glimpses of the Arab walls, medieval plazas, monasteries and the Palacio Real (Royal Palace), built on the site of the older Muslim Alcázar. The lively Puerta del Sol, still the beating heart of the city, marks the eastern edge of Habsburg Madrid.

The Bourbon monarchs of the 18th century fostered the city's expansion further east. They commissioned grand avenues and boulevards, fountains and gateways. Bourbon Madrid is best symbolised by the handsome Paseo del Prado and the banking mansions between it and the Puerta del Sol. Wedged between this monumental part of town and the historic old town are the city's most characterful popular quarters, such as Lavapiés, Chueca and Malasaña.

Modern Madrid grew unrelentingly in all directions from the early 19th century. Uptown Salamanca is an elegant if faded quarter of apartment buildings and sophisticated shops built around a grid of streets bordered by La Castellana and Paseo de Recoletos, the northward extensions of the Prado boulevard. Both are lined with pavement cafés. Since the 1980s, La Castellana has pushed further north, beyond the financial district. Its northern limit is now marked by Las Cuatro Torres, four spectacular architect-designed towers.

Two towers of the Las Cuatro Torres development

## Architecture

Madrid's diverse architecture traces the prevailing styles of the different eras in which it spread outwards. Moving from the centre, one passes from stately 16th-century buildings with wrought-iron balconies, brick facades and stone features, to baroque Bourbon palaces, neoclassical buildings and the elegant Belle Epoque, Art Nouveau

The 19th-century Palacio de Cristal in Retiro Park

and Art Deco styles of the Gran Vía. The severe architecture of Franco's dictatorship, on La Castellana, gave way during the 1990s to a wave of eye-catching flagship architecture and, just as important, restoration of the popular old quarters. Their quiet but colourful tree-lined streets are now as beautiful as the city's grander quarters.

## Modernity and Tradition

Madrid was at the forefront of the dynamic Spain that emerged after Franco's death in 1975, ending 40 years of dictatorship, cultural and intellectual isolation. Once unshakeably conservative and Catholic, Spain today has one of Europe's lowest birth rates, rapidly falling church attendance and legally recognised gay marriage. Twenty five years of economic boom have been followed by the shadow of prolonged economic crisis, during which Madrileños are now rethinking their city's future.

What has endured throughout a century of political upheaval and transitions is the love of exuberant street life. Outside work hours, Madrileños spill on to pavements, pack outdoor cafés and still take the leisurely evening paseo. Conservatively dressed businessmen escort impeccably groomed women, while pensioners play chess or card games in the parks. Locals of all ages crowd into bars and taverns to sip vermouth or ice-cold beer or *vino tinto*, and to munch on tapas, such as *tortilla española*.

The city clings to *castizo* (working-class Madrileño) traditions too. Las Ventas bullring is a shrine for aficionados of bullfighting *(la corrida)* while local *fiestas* such as San Isidro, a celebration of the city's patron saint, are as affectionately enjoyed as in small Spanish towns.

'Nueve meses de invierno y tres de infierno...' ('Nine months of winter and three of hell...'). This much-quoted proverb about Madrid's climate is almost a historic joke now thanks to air-conditioning and central heating. Madrid today embraces its extremes easily. The shifts between freezing winters and scorching summers, elegant boulevards and characterful backstreets are marked yet easy ones. There are

## The Castizo Spirit

Madrid's flea market, the Rastro, is the mecca of *castizo* culture. Like London's Cockney culture, it is famed for its quick and witty wordplay and its strong community spirit. *Castizo* culture dates back to the 18th century, when the ruling classes began to adopt French styles, and in response the local people developed a swaggering chutzpah and an exaggerated accent deliberately incomprehensible to an outsider. The castizo spirit survives today in its language, which is old-fashioned and formal, but full of puns, double meanings, *piripos* (flirtatious compliments) and verbal pirouettes.

other contrasts too: Madrid remains a city of barrios, or quarters, each of which revels in its own individuality. Historic traditions are as celebrated as contemporary arts, best known through Pedro Almodóvar's films, which have captured the city's quirky personality so well. It is this kaleidoscopic mix which makes Madrid such a memorable place for any visitor.

## Options from Madrid

Madrid is the perfect base for exploring Castile. A trio of Unesco-honoured cities lie within an hour's journey.

A torero at Las Ventas

Toledo, Spain's former capital, set on a mound above a river moat, keeps an outstanding architectural legacy from its Christian, Jewish and Muslim medieval culture. Segovia, once a royal stronghold, has a fairy-tale castle, a 2,000-year-old Roman aqueduct and wonderful Romanesque churches. The city of Ávila, the birthplace of St Teresa, may be viewed from its perfectly preserved medieval city wall.

Closer to Madrid is the royal monastery of El Escorial, a mausoleum and palace built by Felipe II, from which he governed the Spanish empire. Aranjuez and Chinchón, to the south of Madrid, may be visited together in a day by car. One is an ornamental royal palace and the other a pleasant Castilian country town.

# A BRIEF HISTORY

Though prehistoric remains from the Palaeolithic, Neolithic and Bronze Ages have been unearthed in the Manzanares valley, Madrid was a quiet farming town prior to its sudden elevation to capital city in 1561.

Over many centuries Madrid's future significance would have been hard to foresee. The Romans dominated and settled large parts of the Iberian peninsula, but left nothing of consequence here. Muslim armies invaded the peninsula in AD711 via North Africa and overran most of what is Spain today within a decade. If Madrid played any role in these pivotal events, no record remains, though it is clear from the Arabic origin of Madrid's name 'place of many springs', variously recorded as Magerit, Mayrit or Magrit, that their appreciation of its endless supply of snow and spring water underlay the growth of the early town.

During three and a half centuries of Muslim rule the local army built a full-scale fortified palace, or *alcázar*, on the west-facing heights of Madrid commanding the Manzanares valley.

After several unsuccessful skirmishes, the Christian forces of Alfonso VI captured Madrid in 1083, and the *alcázar* became a fort of the crown of Castile. During a counter-offensive in 1109, the town was overrun by the Muslims, but the Christianised fortress held and Madrid became a secure walled Christian town. Nonetheless, the Muslim community and later its lifestyle continued

## Mudéjar style

*Mudéjar* architecture refers to a style made popular after the Christian reconquest of Spain. Christians employed Muslim craftsmen to construct buildings with intricate carved and painted Moorish decoration.

Fernando and Isabel greet Christopher Columbus

to be an everyday part of life here long after the fall of Granada in 1492.

Meanwhile, Madrid enjoyed brief prominence in 1309 when Ferdinand IV and his Cortes, an early version of parliament, held a formal meeting in the fledgling town. From then on, the kings of Spain began to visit Madrid, where the air was invigorating, the water pure and the hunting excellent.

Fernando and Isabel, the Catholic monarchs whose marriage united the kingdoms of Aragon and Castile, first visited Madrid in 1477. They appreciated the town's loyalty, but cultured Toledo continued secure in its role as Spain's capital.

## Spain's Golden Age

Under Fernando and Isabel, Spain underwent a dramatic transformation. In 1492 the couple presided over the conquest and discovery of the New World. Over the following

century it was to bring great
wealth to Spain from the
newly established American
colonies. Often called the
country's Golden Age, this
was a century of Spanish
political supremacy, accom-
panied by marvels of art and
literature, although the roots
of decline were present in
tensions with the converted
Jews and Muslims, economic inflation and the Inquisition's
censorship of cultural life.

Fernando and Isabel were consummate Spaniards, commit-
ted to the expansion of the crown, closely controlled from
an itinerant court. By contrast, their grandson, who assumed
the throne as Carlos I in 1516, was born in Flanders in 1500
and could barely express himself in Spanish. The first of the
Habsburg dynasty, he packed his retinue with Burgundian and
Flemish nobles.

Soon after his arrival in Spain, he inherited the title of
Holy Roman Emperor, as Carlos V. His responsibilities in
northern Europe kept him busy, away from the royal residences of Toledo, Segovia, Valladolid and Madrid. While the
monarch was away on one of his many trips, revolts broke
out in a number of Spanish cities, including Madrid, where
the rebels occupied the *alcázar* (by then a royal palace). The
insurrection was quashed and its leaders executed, but the
king got the message: he needed to pay more attention to
his Spanish subjects.

## Madrid's Rise to Capital

In 1556, Carlos abdicated in favour of his son, Felipe II –
good news for Spain and even better for Madrid. Felipe

moved the royal court from Toledo to Madrid in 1561, converting a town of fewer than 15,000 people into the capital of the world's greatest empire. Madrid expanded in a largely improvised way, increasing nearly eight-fold in population in just 50 years. Spain's fortunes as a whole were more volatile. Felipe II took credit for a rousing naval victory at Lepanto against the Turks, but less than two decades later Spain was subjected to the humiliating defeat of its 'invincible' armada, at the hands of Sir Francis Drake. Felipe II's greatest architectural legacy was El Escorial, his severe palace, monastery and library in the foothills of the Sierra de Guadarrama, northwest of Madrid.

Felipe's son, Felipe III was to hold court in Valladolid for several years, though eventually he returned to Madrid. It was he who ordered the construction of the five-storey Plaza Mayor later rebuilt three times, but still a magnificent main

A public spectacle in the Plaza Mayor, around 1700

square for staging public events. Nearby the 17th-century Plaza de la Villa, little changed today, reveals that Madrid was at last taking itself seriously as a city.

The death of Carlos II, heirless, in 1700 sparked a war over the Spanish succession, which resulted in the enthronement of the Bourbon Felipe V. When Madrid's *alcázar* burned down in 1734, with the loss of many art treasures, Felipe seized the opportunity to build a lavish new royal palace, today's Palacio Real. The building is still used for government and royal ceremonies, although the royal family lives in the Palacio de la Zarzuela, just to the northwest of Madrid.

Madrid still honours the memory of Carlos III, the most popular Bourbon king, who ruled from 1759 to 1788. He installed public fountains and laid out the Paseo del Prado, he worked hard to pave and lamplight humbler streets and to eradicate crime.

Spain again became a battleground in the early 1800s, with British forces taking on Napoleon's troops in the Peninsular War, called the War of Independence by Spaniards. Napoleon invaded Spain in March 1808 and invested his brother, Joseph, as King José I. On 2 May 1808, Madrid rose up against the interloper. The war went on murderously but inconclusively for six years. Finally, with the help of the British under the Duke of Wellington, the Spanish expelled the occupying forces, who left behind a trail of destruction. In part, Joseph Bonaparte had meant well, he built so many plazas that Madrileños nicknamed him El Rey Plazuelas – but the people loathed a government imposed from abroad.

## Decline and Decadence
The son of Carlos IV, Fernando VII, was seated on his rightful throne in Madrid's Palacio Real in 1814. But the War of Independence and the repercussions of the French Revolution

Nationalist troops advance on Madrid

had helped to create in Spain the nucleus of a liberal nationalist party. Power struggles ensued.

The spirit of liberalism prevalent in Europe was tardy in reaching Spain. After many reverses, a democratic constitution was finally proclaimed and constitutional monarchy was instituted in 1874. Alongside this the Spanish–American War of 1898 marked the final collapse of the Spanish empire of the Golden Age, steadily whittled to insignificance. King Alfonso XIII inaugurated the Madrid Metro and University City, but he was undone by the chronic unrest of his subjects. Neither constitutional government nor dictatorship proved workable, and in 1931 the king went into exile following anti-royalist results in municipal elections.

## The Civil War

The 1931 general elections created the Second Republic. Bitter ideological conflicts divided parties and produced factions,

## War statistics

The Civil War ended with some 700,000 combatants dead; another 30,000 were executed or assassinated; an estimated 15,000 civilians were killed in air raids. Only now are communal tombs being opened.

and the church became heavily involved. For the next few years the pendulum of power oscillated between left and right as displaced conservative powers worked hard to undermine the Republic.

In 1936, a large section of the army under General Francisco Franco rose against the government. On Franco's side (the Nationalists) were monarchists, conservatives, the Catholic Church and the right-wing Falangists. United against him were republicans, liberals, socialists, communists and anarchists. The Civil War developed into one of the great ideological causes of the 20th century. Many Europeans, not always aware of the origins of the struggle, saw the Civil War as a crucial conflict between democracy and dictatorship; or from the other side, as a conflict between law and order and the forces of social revolution and chaos. Madrid remained in Republican hands for most of the war though under siege until March 1939.

Hardship, hunger and cultural isolation dogged the 40-year dictatorship following Generalísimo Franco's victory. Although he kept Spain neutral in World War II, some Spaniards enlisted for Hitler, and Nazi planes bombed civilians in the Basque town of Guernica. Finally, Spain was admitted to the United Nations (UN) in 1955 and from the early 1960s, when tourism took off, an economic transformation began that would have profound effects on national identity.

When Franco died in 1975, the coronation of Franco's designated successor, Juan Carlos, the grandson of Alfonso XIII, ushered in the so-called 'transition' to parliamentary democracy. The king's commitment to democracy, which pleasantly surprised many people, brought Spain into line with the rest of Western Europe and assured it of future membership in the European Economic Community (now the European Union). In the early 1980s Madrid won a place on the cultural map thanks to its *movida* (see page 10), a street-wise cultural explosion that rejected the stagnation of the Franco era.

## Modern Spain

Under Felipe González, Socialist prime minister from 1982 to 1996, Spain stepped onto the world stage. Symbolically, in 1992, Barcelona hosted the Olympic Games, Seville the World Expo, and Madrid was European Capital of Culture. González was credited by many as a principal architect of the new Spain, but his party lost power after incessant charges of corruption. In 1996, José María Aznar formed a conservative (Partido

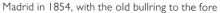

Madrid in 1854, with the old bullring to the fore

Popular) government. During his eight years in power a spectacular property boom began, fuelled by town halls' local control of planning.

On 11 March 2004, three days before national elections, 10 bombs tore through three commuter trains at Atocha station in Madrid. Some 201 people were killed and around 1,500 injured. Aznar's attempt to blame the attack on Basque separatists was one of various factors that created a swing of votes towards the Socialists (PSOE), led by José Luís Zapatero. His reforming spirit in dealing with corruption, ensuring modern civil rights and encouraging a federal state was widely supported, but dragged down by the government's delayed reaction to growing economic crisis. By 2011, when elections returned the Partido Popular to power, Spain's unemployment rate was the highest in Europe and still rising.

Dynamic design at Madrid airport

Yet for all its change of profile in austere times Madrileños have shown that economic clouds on the horizon cannot dampen their native wit and zest for life. As the city's policy makers become pivotal to Europe's future, they have also revealed that Madrid remains as ambitious to step up and play a bigger role on the world stage as it was 450 years earlier.

# Historical Landmarks

**900–400BC** Celtic tribes settle and mix with indigenous Iberians.

**206BC** End of Carthaginian rule in Spain.

**AD711** Islamic armies invade Spain.

**852** Muslims found settlement of Magerit.

**996** Madrid conquered by Castile.

**1109** Muslims unsuccessfully storm Madrid. Madrid wins town status.

**1309** Royal Parliament (Cortes) held in Madrid.

**1469** Marriage of Fernando and Isabel unites Aragón and Catalonia with Castile to create a unified Spain.

**1492** Moors defeated in Granada; Muslims and Jews expelled.

**1561** Felipe II establishes capital in Madrid, replacing Toledo.

**1606** Madrid renamed capital of Spain.

**1701–13** War of Spanish Succession.

**1808–14** Peninsular War; Joseph Bonaparte becomes king.

**1835** State confiscation and sale of monasteries and convents.

**1874** Restoration of Bourbon monarchy.

**1931** Second Republic created after municipal elections.

**1936–9** Spanish Civil War ends in Franco dictatorship.

**1975** Franco dies, Juan Carlos becomes king.

**1979–80** Catalonia and the Basque country and other regions gain federal rights to a new constitution.

**1986** Spain joins European Community (now European Union).

**1992** Madrid is European Capital of Culture.

**1997** Conservative Partido Popular's José María Aznar elected.

**2004** Ten bombs kill 201 on Madrid commuter trains. Socialist PSOE party elected. Spain's Crown Prince Felipe marries Letizia Ortiz.

**2007** Law of Historic Memory permits opening of Civil War graves.

**2011** The Indignados (Outraged) occupation of Puerta del Sol in May, in protest at 50 percent youth unemployment, attracts world attention.

**2012** Catalonia's government announces a referendum on the region's independence from Spain, in 2014.

# WHERE TO GO

Lying at the heart of the sprawling modern city, the old and new parts of Madrid of greatest interest to visitors are remarkably compact. Old Madrid, the city of the Habsburgs, covers a small area that extends east from the Río Manzanares to Puerta del Sol. Almost all of it can be covered in a day or two, including the lengthy visit to the magnificent Royal Palace. The museums that are home to Spain's great art collections, clustered on the Paseo del Prado, are equally worthy of exploration. For art lovers, this area Spain's so-called 'Golden Triangle of Art', between central Plaza de Cibeles and Atocha railway station, may be the area where they want to spend most time. Those who enjoy exploring the city's backstreets may like to explore popular old barrios (city quarters) such as Lavapiés, Chueca and Malasaña. Salamanca is more sedate, and Gran Vía is the turn-of-the-20th-century avenue that connects central to western Madrid.

## OLD MADRID

Old Madrid, the area spreading outward from the Plaza Mayor, is the city's most historic quarter. After Madrid became the seat of the royal court, this area grew rapidly in the 16th and 17th centuries. Its streets are full of atmospheric *tascas* (bars) and restaurants, churches, aristocratic palaces and major sights like the Palacio Real (Royal Palace), Plaza Mayor, Puerta del Sol and Convento de las Decalzas Reales, Madrid's most important convent.

Enough buildings and monuments from medieval Madrid remain, along with its street layout, to evoke its atmosphere. It's

Monument to Alfonso XII, Parque del Retiro

The Plaza Mayor

palpable in the narrow streets that meander south from the Calle Mayor and quiet plazas in and around the area of La Latina.

## Plaza Mayor

The porticoed **Plaza Mayor** ❶, an architectural symphony of bold but balanced lines, is one of Spain's best-loved squares. Broad arcades surround a cobbled rectangle 200m long and 100m wide (656ft x 328ft). Originally built at the beginning of the 17th century, based on the style of Juan de Herrera (Felipe II's architect, responsible for El Escorial; see page 70), the square we know today, with slate roofs, slender towers and facades of brick and stone dates from 1790–1854. The Plaza Mayor may be entered by any of nine archways. Once it was the scene of pageants, markets, theatre festivals, bullfights, religious processions and even trials and executions during the Spanish Inquisition – residents with access to any of the 400 balconies overlooking the square used to sell tickets for such events. A statue of Felipe III occupies a place of honour, and the Casa de la Panadería (bakery) is decorated with colourful modern frescoes. You can take in the elegant architectural ensemble from a seat at one of the outdoor cafés or during a night-time stroll.

Leading out of each of the Plaza's arched doorways are narrow, winding streets or stairs. The most famous of these is **Cava San Miguel**, in the southwestern quarter, lined with shops, taverns and *mesones* (cave-like bars). If you head for Calle Mayor on the western side, you'll come first to the **Mercado de San Miguel** (Mon, Wed–Sun 10am–midnight, Thur–Sat 10am–2am) a beautiful Art Nouveau food market, polemically revamped as a pricy emporium for buying and sampling food and wine.

## Plaza de la Villa

Further along Calle Mayor is Madrid's oldest square, **Plaza de la Villa ❷**, once the seat of the city's government. The 15th-century Gothic **Casa y Torre de los Lujanes** (House and Tower of the Lujanes) has an imposing stone portal and *mudéjar* tower. **Casa de Cisneros**, on the south side of the square, was built in the mid-16th century by a nephew of the inquisitor and warrior, Cardinal Cisneros, and is a fine example of the delicate, ornate style of architecture known as Plateresque. The **Ayuntamiento** (City Hall) dates from the Habsburg era, with the towers and slate spires characteristic of the 17th-century official buildings common in this district of Madrid.

Casa de Panadería detail

Beyond Calle Mayor, crossing Calle de Bailén, is **Parque Emir Mohammed I**, where you can see fragments of the old Moorish wall that encircled the Magerit settlement.

## La Morería and La Latina

South of Plaza de la Villa and Calle de Segovia is the old Moorish district, **La Morería**, where the intense traffic and bustle of Madrid suddenly subsides. The quiet and pretty square, **Plaza de la Paja** (Straw Square), was the commercial focus of the city in the days before the Plaza Mayor. On the south side of the plaza, with its entrance around the other side, is **Iglesia de San Andrés**, splendidly restored (daily 7.45am–1pm, 6.30–8pm). Inside is the **Capilla del Obispo**, marking the original burial place of Madrid's patron saint.

Adjoining it is the **Museo de los Origenes ❸** (Plaza de San Andrés; Tue–Fri 9.30am–8pm, Sat–Sun and hols 10am–2pm; Aug 9.30am–2pm; free), built within the restored shell of the palace of the Vargas family, for whom Isidro worked as a labourer. Built around a large patio planted with local sierra trees and flowers, the museum gives a lively overview of Madrid when it was a farming town, using fossils, 3D audiovisuals, artefacts and architectural models. The rooms dedicated to San Isidro show paintings

Iglesia de San Andrés

and other images that tell how his legend developed.

Just southwest of here is the formidable mid-18th century **Real Basílica de San Francisco el Grande** ❹ (Basilica of St Francis of Assisi; Tue–Fri 10.30am–12.30pm and 4–8pm, Sat 10.30am–12.30pm, 4–6pm; Aug daily am and pm; charge). When Madrid's most important friary was rebuilt in neoclassical style, a dome was added with an inner diameter of more than 31m (100ft), larger than

Browsing at the Rastro

that of the cupola of St Paul's in London. Oversized statues of the apostles in white marble are stationed around the rotunda, and seven richly ornamented chapels fan out from the centre. The church's paintings include works by Goya, Ribera and Zurburán.

East of Plaza San Andrés is a closely packed network of animated alleys and streets: among them, **Cava Baja**, **Cava Alta** ❺, Calle Almendro and Calle del Nuncio. They are home to craft shops and, increasingly, bars or eateries inside old taverns. The barrio was one of Madrid's classic working-class areas and is at its most lively on Sunday mornings when **El Rastro** fleamarket (see page 90) fills a warren of streets entered from Calle de Toledo, a lively thoroughfare that leads back up to the Plaza Mayor.

On Calle de Toledo stands the **Colegiata de San Isidro** (daily 8.30am–2pm and 6–8pm). Built by the Jesuits in the early 17th century, this church was modelled on that of the Gesu in Rome, and between 1885 and 1993, was Madrid's cathedral. It remains so today in many Madrileños' hearts. San Isidro keeps many relics, including the revered remains of the city's patron saint, San Isidro Labrador, and a Virgin wearing a military sash awarded by Franco.

## Palacio Real

The **Palacio Real** ❻ (Royal Palace; daily 10am–6pm, Apr–Sept until 8pm; charge), just west of the Plaza de Oriente, was built in the 18th century on the site of the medieval wooden *alcázar* destroyed by fire in 1734. The new grey stone palace, commissioned by Bourbon king Felipe V, was completed in 1755. Set among formal gardens on a bluff overlooking the Manzanares valley, this imperious residence is loaded with art and history.

Guided and self-guided tours of the palace take in only a fraction of the 2,000 rooms (more than any other palace

The Palacio Real

in Europe), but many of its
highlights. You can also see
the formal Changing of the
Royal Guard on the first
Wednesday of every month
at noon (excluding Aug–Sept
and during bad weather).
The first feature visitors see
is the immense **Plaza de la
Armería**, which overlooks
the valley west of Madrid.
The entrance to the palace
is via the main staircase –

Royal guards on parade

bright, airy and ceremonious beneath an arched ceiling. Each
step is a single slab of marble. The Salón de los Halberdiers
contains remarkably well-preserved ancient Flemish and
Spanish tapestries. The walls of the **Salón del Trono** (Throne
Room) are covered by red velvet and mirrors in matching gilt
frames. Its ceiling was painted by Tiepolo in 1764. The conversation antechamber, contributed by Carlos III, has four handsome portraits by Goya.

The apartments of Carlos III consist of one lavish room after
another. The outstanding **Salón de Gasparini** is named after
the artist, Matias Gasparini of Naples, who mobilised stone-
cutters, sculptors, glass-blowers, clockmakers, silversmiths,
cabinet-makers and embroiderers to produce this stunning
example of the rococo style, in which floor, walls and ceiling
swirl with special effects. The **Sala de Porcelana** (Porcelain
Room) is an almost-overwhelming display of porcelain, incorporating over 1,000 18th-century pieces from the factory that
then stood in the Retiro Park.

The regal, extravagant **Comedor de Gala** (Ceremonial
Dining Room), built for the wedding of Alfonso XII and his
second wife, María Cristina, in 1879, seats 145 guests. Notice

Inside the Cathedral

the 15 chandeliers, 10 candelabra and 18th-century Chinese porcelain jars along walls hung with Brussels tapestries.

Two highlights for many visitors are the early Hapsburg **Botica Real** (Royal Pharmacy) and **Armería Real** (Royal Armoury). Built in 1594, the pharmacy's cupboards line two rooms with matching glass-and-porcelain apothecary jars. The **Armería Real** (Royal Armoury) displayed authentic battle flags, trophies, shields and weapons, a collection regarded as one of the finest of its type in the world. In warm weather leave time for a stroll around the royal gardens: the formal **Jardines de Sabitini** and wooded **Campo del Moro** (entrance Po Virgen del Puerto, opening hours as for the Palacio Real).

## Almudena Cathedral

Adjacent to the palace is the **Catedral de Nuestra Señora de la Almudena** (daily 9am–9pm; closed during mass), which was finished in 1993, more than 350 years after the cornerstone was laid. The cathedral is constructed on the site of Muslim Magerit, but its most historic surviving feature is the 16th-century image of the Virgen de la Almudena, patroness of Madrid, which is kept in the crypt. Guided tours (Mon–Sat 10am–2.30pm; charge) include the climb up to the dome.

In May 2004, the cathedral hosted its first royal wedding, that of Prince Felipe of Asturias and former journalist Letizia Ortiz.

## Plaza de Oriente and Opera

The Royal Palace's front facade overlooks the stately **Plaza de Oriente**, lined with statues of Spanish kings and queens, and the **Teatro Real** ❼, Madrid's opera house. A guided visit (daily 10.30am–1pm, every 30 minutes, takes 1 hour; charge) takes in the Teatro's opulent salons and the auditorium which was built over a small river, giving excellent acoustics, but construction problems. Behind the opera house in Plaza Isabel II, underground inside the Metro station, you can see the excavated aqueduct, channelling and wash house fed by the river.

A couple of blocks away stands the **Real Monasterio de la Encarnación** ❽ (Convent of the Incarnation; opening hours as for the Monasterio de las Descalzas Reales; charge, joint ticket available), on the small plaza of the same name. Founded in 1611 by Margarita de Austria, this convent's most fascinating feature is the reliquary room, containing saints' bones and other body parts in gilded cabinets. A small phial

## Drama at the Opera

The Teatro Real has had a chequered past. Built on the site of the Plaza de Oriente's wash house, it opened with a performance of Donizetti's *La Favorita* in 1850, on the birthday of Queen Isabel II, who was an opera fanatic. However, it was closed only 75 years later, when it was found that the stream running beneath it had brought its foundations to the point of collapse. Used as a gunpowder arsenal during the Civil War, the theatre was left closed during Franco's regime – he disliked opera – until it re-opened as a concert hall in 1965. It finally re-opened again, after a decade-long and extravagantly budgeted restoration, in 1999.

of San Pantaleón's blood kept there mysteriously liquefies on the afternoon of 26 July every year. In the 18th-century church, you may hear the nuns pray or sing, but you'll never see them; they are cloistered behind the grillwork.

Nearby is the **Monasterio de las Descalzas Reales** ❾ (Royal Barefoot Franciscans; Tue–Sat 10am–2pm and 4–6.30pm, Sun and hols 10am–3pm, guided tour only; charge, joint ticket available with the Convento de la Encarnación). Founded by Princess Juana de Austria, the daughter of Carlos V, in 1566, this palace was transformed into a convent by the architect responsible for El Escorial. The convent, supported by wealthy patrons, accepted only nuns of the highest nobility until the beginning of the 18th century. The sisters brought with them spectacular works of art set aside originally as their marriage dowries. Until 30 years ago, the convent was completely cloistered and no visits allowed. Today, Franciscan nuns – a maximum of 33 (the age of Jesus when he died) – remain on the premises, but stay out of sight during visiting hours.

The convent's finest feature is its theatrical granite stairway, splashed with splendid 17th-century frescoes from floor to ceiling. On the second floor are rooms with heavy timbered ceilings whose walls are covered with works of art, mostly of religious or royal significance. In one hall hang a dozen splendid 17th-century tapestries based on original Rubens drawings. The museum also contains outstanding paintings by Titian, Brueghel the Elder and Zurbarán, fleetingly pointed out as you pass through the galleries.

### Churches galore

There are more than 200 churches in Madrid. In the Spanish context they are relatively modern, but include fine examples of Mudéjar and Baroque work.

## Puerta del Sol

**Plaza Puerta del Sol** ❿ is Madrid's busiest plaza and for centuries has been the heart of the city. It also marks the transition between Habsburg

Puerta del Sol and the Casa de Correos

Madrid and the city laid out by the Bourbon kings. The original gate that once existed here – originally the eastern gate of the Muslim town – was torn down in 1570. Ten streets converge on the plaza. 'Kilometre Zero', a metal plaque set into the pavement below the clock tower, is the point from which distances from Madrid in Spain and Latin America are measured.

The neoclassical brick building below the clock tower, the **Casa de Correos** dating from 1768, houses the regional government. Thousands of Madrileños gather here for a New Year's Eve ritual. They each swallow a dozen grapes while the clock atop the building strikes midnight, a ritual said to bring good luck for the coming year.

Almost lost in the bustle of the Puerta del Sol is a small statue based on Madrid's coat of arms, which depicts a bear leaning against a madroño tree (an arbutus, or strawberry tree). The bear is a symbol of Madrid, and the strawberry tree one of the sierra's most distinctive plants. Whatever time of day you visit this hectic Plaza, you will find it buzzing not only with visitors, but also, often, buskers and locals sharing news and views.

## Huertas and Santa Ana

Southeast of Puerta del Sol lie **Plaza Santa Ana** and Calle de las Huertas, both today lined with restaurants and bars. Once the area had bullfighting associations: bullfighter Manolete was a regular at the Reina Victoria hotel, now the Me Hotel, on Plaza Santa Ana. The square itself is named after the convent that stood here till it disappeared in the 1830s. Also on the square, on the site of an earlier open-air *corral*, is the historic **Teatro Español**, while at Plaza Santa Ana 6 is Cervecería Alemana, where writers Ernest Hemingway and Lillian Hellman used to hang out.

Reached off the southern side of Plaza Santa Ana, **Calle de las Huertas**, now pedestrianised, has literary quotes set into paving stones in honour of the great authors of the Golden Age and later periods, who lived here close to the theatres where their plays were performed. Not far away, you can visit the **Casa Museo Lope de Vega** ⓫ (Calle Cervantes 11; Tue–Sun 10am–3pm; free; book ahead). The home of Spain's most famous dramatist is beautifully restored as a museum of 17th-century life.

Bear and strawberry tree, symbol of Madrid, in Puerta del Sol

## Lavapiés

South of Plaza Santa Ana and Antón Martin Metro station is the sloping quarter of **Lavapiés** (literally 'wash

Facades in Lavapiés

feet'), legendarily named after a fountain used for washing feet. In the 15th century, this was the old Jewish quarter, which has left its mark in winding and twisting streets, the remains of a synagogue under the church of San Lorenzo, and the saintly Catholic street names given when the Jews were expelled. Still one of Madrid's most lively working-class districts, this quarter is now home to a thriving alternative arts scene.

At the heart of the area is lively **Plaza de Lavapiés**. All around the square and in the streets running off it are interesting bars and restaurants. Today many are exotic – there are excellent Arab cafés and an increasing selection of Indian and Turkish ones – but older locals remain loyal to their traditional foods, such as *cocido*, Madrid's one-pot chickpea stew, *caracoles* (snails), *callos* (tripe) and oreja (fried strips of pig's ear).

On the eastern side of Lavapiés spreads **El Rastro**, Madrid's famous Sunday flea market.

## Calle de Alcalá to Plaza de Cibeles

East of Puerta del Sol are the city's 18th-century quarters engineered by the Bourbon monarchs. **Calle de Alcalá**, once the city's main financial district, leads to the Plaza de Cibeles and the Paseo del Prado. Its spacious boulevards, grand plazas and fountains are interspersed with imposing 18th-century blocks that house the head offices or branches of more than 100 banks, plus insurance companies, and, on nearby Plaza de la Lealtad, the Bolsa de Comercio (Stock Exchange).

On Calle de Alcalá is the **Real Academia de Bellas Artes de San Fernando ⑫** (Tue–Sun and hols 9am–3pm, Mon and hols 9am–2.30pm; charge; www.rabasf.insde.es) – the Royal Academy, home to a celebrated collection of Goya's paintings, including *Burial of the Sardine*, and a superb self-portrait of the artist in his old age. Works by Velázquez, Murillo and Rubens are also represented along with a magnificent collection of paintings by Zurbarán, rivalling that of the Prado.

Just before the junction of Calle de Alcalá with the Paseo del Prado sits the **Círculo de Bellas Artes ⑬**, a cultural centre (entrance Calle Marqués de Casa Riera 2; non-members admitted for a small charge), built in 1927. The centre's café, replete with chandeliers, vast windows and a grand marble nude by Moisés Huerta (1910), is a favourite among the city's cultural crowd. The entrance fee includes a visit to the rooftop Azotea for spectacular 365-degree views from the seventh floor.

The point where Calle Alcalá crosses the old city's main north-south artery is a

Cupola of the Metropolis Building on Calle Alcalá

The goddess and her chariot on Plaza de Cibeles

huge, noisy and polluted – yet still impressive – crossroads called **Plaza de Cibeles**. The central fountain shows Cybele, the Greek goddess of fertility and symbol of the city, serenely settled in a chariot pulled by two lions. On the south-eatern side, the **Palacio de Comunicaciones**, inaugurated in 1919, one of Europe's grandest post offices, has been revamped as the city hall. Located on the southwest corner of Plaza de Cibeles is the **Banco de España** (Bank of Spain) and on the northeast corner is the **Casa de America**, a Latin American cultural centre housed in the plush 19th-century **Palacio de Linares ⑭** (Sat–Sun hourly, 11am–1pm, guided tour; charge; www.casaamerica.es).

## PASEO DEL PRADO

The elegant **Paseo del Prado**, the southern kilometre of the great 5km (3-mile) long Paseo de la Castellana, is home to one of the world's most impressive cluster of art museums: the Prado, the Thyssen Bornemisza, the Reina Sofía and the smaller CaixaForum. Visitors can stroll down the Paseo's shady boulevard, designed for carriages, repair to the Botanical Garden or explore smaller nearby museums.

## Museo del Prado

The **Museo Nacional del Prado** ⓯ (daily 10am–8pm, Sun and hols 7pm; charge; advanced booking tel: 902-107 077; www.museodelprado.es), houses one of the world's largest and most prestigious painting collections. Apart from its Spanish treasures, it includes great works from both the Italian and Flemish schools. The immense collection, ranging from the 12th–19th century, was collected and commissioned by Spain's Habsburg and Bourbon kings, private patrons, and convents and monasteries around the country.

The CaixaForum and its vertical wall-garden

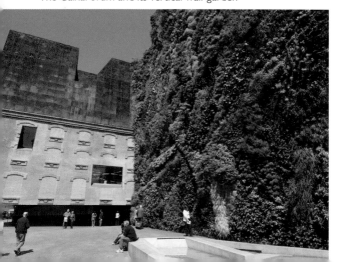

Despite its greatness, the museum came about somewhat by chance. In the 18th century, Carlos III commissioned the architect Juan de Villanueva, draughtsman of the royal palace, to design this neoclassical building as a museum of natural history next to a botanical garden. After some eventful delays (Napoleon's invasion badly damaged the building), it was

Inside the Prado

decided to use it instead for art. It was inaugurated in 1819 and in 1868 it became El Museo del Prado.

Recent modernisation has included a new wing for temporary shows. Pritzker prize-winning Spanish architect Rafael Moneo designed the extension in the former cloisters of the neighbouring Jeronimite church opposite, with splendid contemporary wrought iron doors by Basque artist Cristina Iglesias.

The nearby Casón del Buen Retiro, which used to house later -19th-century paintings (and later Picasso's *Guernica*, at his own request for it to hang in the Prado), is now the museum's study centre. Long-scheduled but polemical works to redesign the Paseo del Prado itself to create a so-called 'Paseo del Arte', allowing easier pedestrian passage between the Thyssen, Prado and Reina Sofía museums, are currently on hold.

The Prado owns around 8,600 paintings, but at present can only display about 2,000 of them (the overflow is either in storage or on loan to museums around Spain and elsewhere). The result is a stunning collection of master works considered unique primarily for the Habsburgs' collecting tastes, which were unusually broad for the period, cutting across nationalities and cultures.

Visitors often opt for condensed highlights – the illustrated guide sheet facilitates this – and so artworks here are ordered by nationality of schools rather than as a comprehensive tour of the museum.

## Highlights of the Prado

**SPANISH**: The greatest Spanish artist of the Golden Age, **Diego Velázquez y Silva** (1599–1660), was hired by King Felipe IV and became an amazingly perceptive court painter and portraitist. The Prado keeps nearly three-quarters of his paintings. The royal family is featured in his seminal work, **Las Meninas** (*The Maids of Honour*). The artist painted himself, palette in hand, at the side of his own masterpiece, in a sense part of the family.

Another vast, unforgettable canvas here is Surrender of Breda, commemorating a Spanish victory over Dutch forces in 1625. Chivalry and exhaustion, the array of upraised lances, and the burning landscape communicate a profound pathos, as does his study of Mars, the god of war, hanging close by. Elsewhere are portraits of the high and the mighty, interspersed with studies of ordinary mortals. Other great works include *Las Hilanderas* (*The Spinners*) and *Los Borrachos* (*The Drunkards*).

**Francisco de Goya** (1746–1828), another great court painter, had a tumultuous, wildly varied career. His works in the Prado, which trace an extraordinary lifelong evolution of style, form the largest Goya ensemble in the world. Born

Diego de Acedo (1644), by Velázquez, in the Prado

Goya's *La Maja Desnuda*, radically modern when first revealed

in Aragon, Goya fled Zaragoza in 1763 for the anonymity of Madrid where he went on to become the king's principal artist. Among the Prado's paintings is **La Maja Desnuda** *(The Naked Maja)*, one of Spain's first nudes. Rumours of a scandalous affair between Goya and the Duchess of Alba have long been assumed though art historians now suggest the *maja* – a Madrileño name for an attractive woman – was Spanish politician Godoy's lover. Goya's most celebrated royal portrait, *The Family of Carlos IV* is daringly honest; only the royal children look remotely attractive. On another level his large canvas, **The Executions of the 3rd of May**, one of history's most powerful protest pictures, depicts the shooting of Spanish patriots by the French in 1808. Goya witnessed this tragedy of the War of Independence from his cottage, and went to the scene to sketch the victims by moonlight. His most mature harrowing 'black paintings', done at home, in old age, when he is said to have lost his sanity (*see Saturn Devouring One of His Sons*), are extraordinarily modern in conception and form a focal point in a dramatically lit gallery.

**El Greco** (1541–1614), born in Crete and long a resident in Italy, became a consummate Spanish painter. He worked in Toledo, his adopted city, for 37 years, toiling at the immense, intensely personal, religious canvases, typically in blacks, yellows and deep mauves, with elongated figures that are his hallmark. *Knight with His Hand on Chest*, an early portrait, is a study of a deep-eyed caballero (gentleman) in black. It is signed, in Greek letters, 'Domenikos Theotokopoulos', the artist's real name. The Prado also has several of El Greco's passionately coloured religious paintings, such as *Adoration of the Shepherds*.

**Francisco de Zurbarán** (1598–1664), a friar and member of the Seville school, combined mysticism and realism. His greatest works are of mythological, religious and historic themes. Monks, priests and saints are portrayed in flowing robes with almost tangible textures. The Prado owns his strained but fascinating battle picture *The Defence of Cádiz Against the English* and his *Still Life*, of a goblet, two vases and a pot emerging from a black background.

**Bartolomé Murillo** (1617–82), Spain's most popular religious artist of his time, depicted Biblical personalities at ease. His tender and classical religious works brought him international fame, although detractors label his work mawkish. Certainly it is an interesting counterpoint that highlights the genius of his contemporary, Velázquez.

**Optical defect**

In the 20th century, some critics wondered whether El Greco's revolutionary elongated figures were the result of astigmatism.

**José Ribera** (c.1591–1652) spent much of his life in Italy, where the Valencia-born artist was known as *lo Spagnoletto* (the little Spaniard). His

Bosch's *The Garden of Earthly Delights*

portraits of saints, hermits and martyrs reveal impeccable drawing skills, composition and keen awareness of the power of light and shadow.

**DUTCH, FLEMISH AND GERMAN:** Hieronymus **Bosch** (c.1450–1516), whom the Spanish call El Bosco, has three masterpieces in the Prado, including the large, extraordinarily detailed triptych **The Garden of Earthly Delights**. Daringly mixing erotic fantasies and apocalyptic nightmares, it portrays the terrors and superstitions of the medieval peasant mind. Bosch's wild hallucinations presage similar psychological explorations 400 years later by Salvador Dalí.

**Peter Paul Rubens** (1577–1640) pursued a career as a diplomat as well as an artist. Of particular note is his huge **Adoration of the Magi**, a brilliant religious extravaganza, and **The Three Graces**, a portrait of fleshy nudes; the woman on the right is said to be Rubens' second wife, Helena.

The finest work of **Rogier van der Weyden** (c.1400–64), the altarpiece *Descent From the Cross*, is on the ground floor. Elsewhere is a famous work by German Renaissance painter **Albrecht Dürer** (1471–1528) – his *Self-Portrait at 26.*

**ITALIAN**: Works by **Titian** (c.1490–1576) include the *Portrait of the Emperor Carlos V.* Depicting Titian's patron in armour, on horseback at the Battle of Mühlberg, it set the standard for court painters for the next century. Titian also produced religious works, but seemed to have no difficulty changing gears to the downright lascivious, as in his *Baccanal*.

The collection of paintings by **Raphaël** (1483–1520) in the Prado was at one point taken lock, stock and barrel to Paris under the orders of Napoleon, but it was soon returned. Centuries of investigation have failed to uncover the identity of *The Cardinal*, Raphael's explosive character study of a subject with fish-like eyes, aquiline nose and cool, thin lips.

Pausing by an abstract by Piet Mondrian, Thyssen-Bornemisza

**Tintoretto** (1518–94) brought Mannerism to Venice. Look for his representations of dramatic biblical stories (originally ceiling paintings) and, on quite another plane, the close-up of a *Lady Revealing her Bosom*.

If you need respite from the vast museum, pop into the neighbouring Jardín Botánico, or head toward Calle Huertas for everyday street life and refreshments.

## Museo Thyssen-Bornemisza

On the opposite side of the Paseo del Prado, in the salmon-coloured Palacio de Villahermosa, is the **Museo Thyssen-Bornemisza** ⑯ (Paseo del Prado 8; Tue–Sun 10am–7pm; charge; www.museothyssen.org). The Thyssen Collection, widely considered to be the greatest private collection after that of England's Queen Elizabeth II, opened in Madrid in 1992. Previously, it hung in Baron Thyssen-Bornemisza's Villa Favorita, at Lugano. An impressive extension to the museum, to house the collection of Thyssen-Bornemisza's fifth wife, Carmen, was opened in 2004.

What makes the collection so interesting is the personal 'eye' behind the 800 paintings on display, dating from the 13th century to the present day. From the 19th and 20th centuries there are carefully chosen examples of work from key movements: the Paris school, German expressionism, Russian avant-garde and 19th century American painting. Among the classical works are stunning paintings by Fra Angélico, Van Eyck, Dürer, Rembrandt, Hals, Titian, Van Dyck and Rubens. The Impressionists are represented by Manet, Monet, Renoir, Gauguin, Toulouse-Lautrec, Cézanne and Van Gogh.

The representation of artists from the second half of the 20th century to the present day includes works by Francis Bacon (*Portrait of George Dyer in a Mirror*, 1968), Robert Rauschenberg, David Hockney, Lucian Freud, Roy Lichtenstein and other pop artists.

## Museo Nacional Centro de Arte Reina Sofía

Among the cluster of museums on the Paseo del Prado, the **Museo Nacional Centro de Arte Reina Sofía ⑰** (Calle de Santa Isabel 52; Mon–Sat 10am–9pm, Sun and hols 10am–7pm; charge, free Mon–Fri after 7pm, Sat after 2.30pm and Sun; www.museoreinasofia.es), is the fastest-growing collection. Housed in an 18th-century hospital, it currently shows its modern art collection in chronological sections, interweaving work by Spanish and non-Spanish artists and ranging from the turn of the 20th century up to the present. The most celebrated work on show is Picasso's monumental *Guernica*, which is displayed behind bullet-proof glass. On display alongside it are the original preparatory sketches and studies. The centre also houses works by Miró, Dalí, Julio González, Juan Gris and Luis Buñuel, and hosts temporary exhibitions.

### Guernica

Painted in 1937, at the height of the Spanish Civil War, Picasso's *Guernica* was commissioned for the Spanish pavilion of the World's Fair in Paris by Luis Buñuel. In April of that year the Luftwaffe, intervening on behalf of Franco, bombed the town of Guernica (Gernika) in the heart of Spain's Basque region, targeting civilians. Rather than dwelling on the political implications, Picasso directed his intense focus on the suffering caused by violence. Blending techniques from cubism and surrealism, he composed a work of enigmatic yet powerful allusions to earlier Iberian and Spanish art. During and after World War II, the painting came to be seen as a universal expression of anti-war sentiment, and it has also served as a banner for the Basque independence movement. Picasso, who died in 1973, bequeathed the painting to Spain, but stipulated that the legacy should only be effected when democracy was re-established. Finally it was brought to Madrid in 1981 after Spain discarded dictatorship.

Admiring Picasso's *Guernica* in the Centro de Arte Reina Sofía

## Atocha

Directly across from the Reina Sofía is the **Estación de Atocha**, a lofty iron-and-glass hangar-like affair modelled on London's St Pancras station, occupied by a tropical garden. In March 2004 Atocha was catapulted into the world news following bomb attacks on suburban trains by al-Qaeda. In the wake of the bombings Atocha's local station became a shrine of church candles with messages to the bombs' victims. Today the station keeps an underground monument in which visitors gaze skywards through a giant perspex cylinder engraved with some of the messages left here in 2004 (daily 10am–8pm; free).

## Other Museums

Smaller museums in the vicinity of the Prado include **CaixaForum** ⓲ arts centre housed in an old brick power station (Po del Prado, 36; daily 10am–8pm). Converted by Herzog

The luxuriant Atocha Station

and de Meuron, its intriguing geometric brick facade stands alongside a 24m (78ft) vertical wall-garden planted with tropical vegetation. Southeast of Atocha is the **Real Fábrica de Tapices** ❿ (Royal Tapestry Factory; Calle Fuentarrabía 2; Mon–Fri 10am–2pm, guided visits only; charge; www.realfabricadetapices.com), which still works with most of the original 18th-century machinery. Finally, close to Plaza de Cibeles, the **Museo Nacional de Artes Decorativos** ⓴ (National Museum of Decorative Arts; Tue–Sat 9.30am–3pm, Thur Sept–June 5–8pm, Sun and hols 10am–3pm; charge, free Sun and Thur pm; www.mnartesdecorativos.mcu.es) is a fine collection which includes a spectacular tiled 18th-century Valencian kitchen on the top floor.

## Parque del Retiro

East of the museums is the city centre's major green space, **Parque del Buen Retiro** (daily 6am–10pm, May–Sept until midnight). Until 1868, the park was a royal preserve. Today it is a favourite place for Madrileños to stroll or relax in the sun. The rowing boats (10am–8.00pm or sunset if earlier; charge for 45 min sessions) on **El Estanque**, the park's small central lake, are a big attraction all year round. On the eastern side of the lake a semi-circular stone colonnade makes a majestic backdrop to a bronze **monument to Alfonso XII**, unveiled by his son, Alfonso XIII. The latter survived a bomb attack on the day of his wedding to Queen Victoria's granddaughter, Victoria Eugenia, grandmother of today's King Juan Carlos, thanks to a message carved on a tree in the Retiro.

Other highlights within the park include the **Palacio de Cristal** ㉑ (Crystal Palace; Mon–Sat 10am–6pm, summer until 8pm, Sun and hols 10am–4pm; free), a jewel-like 19th-century greenhouse modelled on London's Crystal Palace, that now houses contemporary art exhibitions; the rose garden, **La Rosaleda**, where the old varieties of roses smell as lovely as they look (the best time to visit is April to June). In the south-west area of the park, the only public statue in Europe dedicated to the devil, **El Angel Caído** (*The Fallen Angel*), depicts the expulsion of the fallen angel, Lucifer, from the Garden of Eden – a neo-Baroque rendering by the sculptor Ricardo Bellver (1885).

Boating on the lake, Parque del Retiro

A stroll in the Jardín
Botánico

## Real Jardín Botánico

A quieter green oasis, next to the Prado, is the **Real Jardín Botánico** ㉒ (Royal Botanical Garden; Plaza de Murillo 2; daily 10am–dusk, Nov–Feb until 6pm, May–Aug until 9pm; charge; www.rjb.csic.es). It was founded 250 years ago and is laid out around centennial trees, fascinating flowers and rare species. The first dahlias in Europe originated here from seeds brought back from Mexico. In 1803, 7,000 packets of dahlia seeds were sent from here to England, France and Italy for propagation.

At the northwest corner of the Retiro is **Puerta de Alcalá**, a monumental triumphal arch surmounted by warrior-angels, honouring Carlos III. Until the late 19th century, this marked the eastern edge of Madrid. Now called the Plaza de la Independencia, the arch or gateway has become a decorative symbol of the city's cultural openness, seen as a monument to its cosmopolitan tolerance.

## RECOLETOS AND CASTELLANA

The **Paseo de Recoletos**, a 19th-century prolongation of the Paseo del Prado, runs from Plaza de Cibeles to Plaza Colón, where it becomes the **Paseo de la Castellana**, Madrid's principal north–south avenue, running up to the city's northern limits. Patrician townhouses and palaces give way to ministry buildings from Franco's period, modern apartment blocks and high-rise offices. Several notable museums are housed in this quarter.

## Around the Paseo de Recoletos

On the eastern side of the Paseo de Recoletos stands the **Museo Arqueológico Nacional**  (National Archeological Museum; Calle de Serrano 13; Tue–Sat 9.30am–8pm, Sun and hols 9.30am–3pm; charge, free Sat after 2.30pm and Sun; www.man.mcu.es). The museum's collection of art and artefacts stretches from Spain's ancient cultures – Greek, Roman and Visigothic – to the Romanesque pilgrimage route. One star exhibit is the *Dama de Elche*, a stone sculpture found in Alicante province in 1897 and thought to be 2,500 years old. The reopening due in 2013 follows five years complete restoration.

The wide Paseo de Recoletos

Outside the museum's front door is an intriguing underground reproduction of the painted prehistoric scenes discovered in a cave in Altamira in northern Spain.

Recoletos has distinct moods by day and night. Calm during the day, on summer nights its *terrazas* – open-air terrace bars – cater for an elegant well-heeled crowd into the early hours. Among the *terrazas* on the Paseo's west side are the quaint retro kiosks of the traditional **Café Gijón** (No. 21), an intellectuals' and artists' haunt for over a century; and atmospheric **Café Espejo** (No. 31). Both stay open all year round.

Puerta de Alcalá

## Colón

**Plaza de Colón** is a large open space where skateboarders gather to practise among hurried businessmen and pram-pushing mothers. An 1885 statue of Christopher Columbus overlooks a larger modern stone monument to the discovery of the New World. Under the square is the **Centro Cultural de la Villa** (City Cultural Centre) where the Teatro Fernán Gómez hosts seasons of jazz, gospel, flamenco and theatre.

## Along the Castellana

About six blocks north and slightly east is the charming **Museo Sorolla** ㉔ (Paseo del

General Martínez Campos 37; Tue–Sat 9.30am–8pm, Sun 10am–3pm; charge, free Sun; www.museosorolla.mcu.es). This mansion was the home and studio of Joaquín Sorolla (1863–1923), the Valencian Impressionist painter. It now displays 300 of his light-filled seaside scenes and landscapes and preserves a small lovingly tended garden.

Back on the Castellana, around five minutes' walk further north, are the ornate domes of the **Museo de Ciencias Naturales** ㉕ (Natural Science Museum; entrance off Calle de José Gutiérrez Abascal 2; Tue–Fri 10am–6pm, Sat 10am–8pm, July–Aug 10am–3pm, Sun 10am–2.30pm; charge; www.mncu.csic.es). The museum is home to giant skeletons and dinosaur replicas as well as interactive, child-orientated displays on the animal kingdom, anthropological and mineral collections.

## SALAMANCA

**Salamanca**, Madrid's most sedate city quarter, lies east of the Castellana. It came into existence in the mid-1880s when the city's growing population made it necessary to expand beyond the old city centre. At its heart, presiding over the junction of Calles Príncipe de Vergara and Ortega y Gasset, and in the plaza that bears his name, is a statue of the character responsible for building the quarter, the Marqués de Salamanca (1806–83), José or 'Pepito' to his friends. A financier, politician, lawyer and patron of the arts, his career, a roller-coaster of fortunes made and lost, ended in ruin in 1867.

Plaza de Toros, Madrid's
bullfighting arena

Before his luck turned for the last time, he developed Salamanca's grid of streets as a residential refuge for the aristocracy away from the city centre. The Marqués also built Madrid's first tramways, which linked Salamanca with the centre of Madrid. The streets planned by him now have a staid, gentle and sometimes faded air, but retain smart shops and good old-fashioned restaurants.

The Marqués's own magnificent palace, long ago taken over as bank offices, stands at no 10 on the Paseo de Recoletos. The area is crossed north to south by three major roads: Calle de Velázquez, Príncipe de Vergara and, closest to the Castellana, **Calle de Serrano**, all important shopping streets.

In its understated way, Serrano is to Madrid what Bond Street is to London or rue du Faubourg-St-Honoré to Paris: designer-label land. Here, top Spanish names such as Loewe, Carolina Herrera and Hoss Intropia do business alongside foreign arrivals like Prada. The streets off or parallel to Serrano continue the high-end international theme. **Calle de José Ortega y Gasset** is home to Kenzo (15), Versace (10), Armani (16), Chanel (14) and Hermés (12), among others.

On the eastern edge of Salamanca is the **Plaza de Toros y Museo Taurino** ㉖ (Bullfighting Ring and Museum; Calle de Alcalá 231; Bullfighting ring daily 10am–6pm, except on day of bullfights; guided tour only; charge; museum Mon–Fri 9.30am–2.30pm; free). Officially called the Plaza de Toros Monumental de Las Ventas, (and also a venue for rock concerts), this is the place to go to see a bullfight if you can get a ticket, or simply to visit the small museum of posters, capes, swords, paintings and photos for those interested in bullfighting culture.

# GRAN VÍA, MALASAÑA AND CHUECA

The Gran Vía, a concrete canyon of American-style shopping and theatre culture, lies north of Old Madrid. It is bordered

## Bullfighting

Like it or loathe it, it is hard to deny the role the *corrida* (bullfight) holds in Spanish culture. If you decide to see a bullfight, it is helpful to under-stand the different phases of the ritual. There are three *tercios* (acts). In the first, the bull is released, and the matador takes stock, making passes with his large pink-and-yellow *capote* (cape). The *picadores* (mounted men armed with wooden poles tipped with a *puya*, a pointed metal head) try to lance the bull behind its neck muscle, causing the bull's head to lower. In the second *tercio*, the *banderilleros* work on foot to plant long sticks, with a barbed end and covered with coloured paper, into the bull's back.

The final *tercio*, the *faena*, sees the matador return, armed with just a dark red cape called a *muleta*. He adjusts his skills to the strength of the bull, with intricate passes. During the *faena*, the band will strike up an accompanying *pasodoble*; but when the matador is ready for the kill, the most dangerous point in the *corrida*, the band stops.

It is then that the matador, *muleta* in his left hand directing the bull's attention away from his body, and sword in his right, will spin over the dangerous right horn, trying to deliver an *espada* (sword) stroke be-tween the shoulder blades and into the heart, for an instant kill.

Madrid's bullfights at Las Ventas bullring in March, April and the first week of October start at 4.30–5pm (Sunday), while from May to August they begin at 7pm. Tickets can be purchased a day in advance, at Las Ventas (tel: 91-356 2200; 9.30am–2.30pm, 4–6.30pm).

on its north side by fashionable Malasaña, Triball and Chueca, which buzz with life by day and night, and on its south side by Centro's narrow streets.

## Gran Vía

The **Gran Vía** (Great Way) was built in three sections, begun in 1910 and completed in the early 1940s, just after the Spanish Civil War. Conceived as a grand east–west avenue, it cut a channel through the crowded, poorer quarters of the city, and was in part designed for crowd control. Until the 1960s it was Madrid's main commercial centre. Still very active, it has many hotels and high street fashion stores.

Gran Vía at night

The three stretches of the avenue are well defined. At its eastern end, nearly all the buildings have Art Nouveau details and carved stone decoration. Alfonso XIII inaugurated the construction of this section in 1910, and it was opened in 1924. This section ends at the Red de San Luís, marked by an olive tree planted at the top of Calle de la Montera, recently pedestrianised. Once a sophisticated shopping street, it is now better known for its prostitutes, and runs down to the Puerta del Sol.

On the opposite side of the Gran Vía the **Edificio Telefónica** (Fuencarral 3; Tue–Sun 11am–8pm; www.espacio.funacion-telefonica.com) augurs the start of brash commercialism. The headquarters of Telefónica, Spain's telecommunications company, was Madrid's highest building (80m/265ft) when erected in 1929. Its red clock still dominates the night skyline. Inside is an art space showing changing shows with an emphasis on new technology

From this point, the Gran Vía's second stretch runs to the **Plaza del Callao** – the square is named after the 1866 battle of Callao, Peru. At night, neon lights and videos flash above the cinemas' placards. This is a good spot for buying Spanish books and CDs at the giant Casa del Libro bookshop (No. 29) or at Central (Postigo de San Martín 8), a playful book emporium with bistro, a children's zone and reading area.

The third section of the avenue, from Plaza del Callao to Plaza de España, begun in 1925, is more modern in character. Hotels, cinemas and hamburger joints predominate.

## Malasaña

North of Callao is **Malasaña**, bordered to the east by Calle de Fuencarral and to the west by the Calle de San Bernardo. Malasaña has changed little in its grid-like layout since it was built in the 18th century. Still a rabbit warren of narrow streets, it has always had a lively street life. Nothing highlights this better than the 1808 uprising against Napoleon's troops (see page 20). In the last 10 years of Franco's rule, it was also the bohemian quarter. These days, by night it still belongs to rock 'n' roll and the city's bar culture. By day it is home to a creative village of small shops offering alternative design, fashion, books, comics, vintage items, fun food and much more.

### Raging bull

On 23 January 1928, a bull being led to the slaughterhouse escaped and ran amok in the Gran Vía, injuring passers-by. Diego Mazquiarán Fortuna, an elderly bullfighter living nearby, tackled the animal and killed it, an act of bravery that brought him contracts in Spain and South America.

Marble statues of heroes Pedro Velarde and Luís Daoíz on Plaza Dos de Mayo

The heart of Malasaña is **Plaza Dos de Mayo** ㉗ (2 May Square). Both it and the surrounding streets are still populated by pensioners born in the area as well as young people attracted by its traditions. Around here, every street has a story. Calle Espíritu Santo (Holy Spirit Street) once bore a wooden cross in memory of a bolt of lightning that set fire to a whorehouse frequented by the disguised Felipe III. One stormy night years later, Felipe IV walked past the cross with his aides. They were set upon by thieves, and it is said that only the sword of one Don Luís de Haro saved the monarch.

One of the city's most beautiful churches is found in the middle of the quarter: the early 17th-century **San Antonio de los Alemanes** ㉘ (Mon–Sat 11am-8pm, Sun and hols 9am–1pm) in Corredera de San Pablo. Inside, the walls are covered by stunning frescoes by Giordano, Cuello and De Ricci.

Further south on Calle de Fuencarral (No. 78) stands the **Museo de Historia** ㉙ (Tue–Fri 9.30am–8pm, Sat–Sun and hols 10am–2pm; free), built over the city's snow wells as an orphanage in the early 18th century. The splendid Baroque doorway, worth a sighting in its own right, depicts San Fernando, patron saint of orphans. Inside, in the basement, it shows a temporary collection of maps and architectural models of Madrid while full refurbishment is planned.

**Calle de Fuencarral** has become Madrid's main hip fashion zone, with dozens of local and international shoe, clothes and tattoo shops mixed in among traditional art suppliers, pharmacies and ironmongers.

To its west there are scores of bars and clubs in Malasaña. Calle San Vicente Ferrer and Calle de la Palma probably have the greatest number. If a cure is what you're after, take a look at the tiles on the walls of the old **Juanse pharmacy** in Calle San Andres, advertising miracle cures for a variety of ailments.

## El Dos de Mayo

At the heart of Malasaña is the **Plaza Dos de Mayo** (2 May Square), formerly an artillery park connected to the 17th-century Palace of Monteleón. On 2 May 1808, during French rule, local people stormed the palace in search of weapons. As French reinforcements arrived, many locals were killed (others were later executed). The most famous victim was Manuela Malasaña, a 17-year-old embroideress who was on her way home when, according to one version of the story, she was stopped and searched by French troops who found a pair of scissors on her. The French, considering these forbidden arms, summarily executed Manuela. The two Spanish heroes of the day were Pedro Velarde and Luís Daoíz, both of whom also died. Their marble statues adorn the centre of the square under the original arched doorway of the palace. The 2 May is still an emotive date in Madrid, when the Plaza Dos de Mayo holds an all-day fiesta.

The Juanse pharmacy in Malasaña

Dating back to the early 1900s, the pharmacy and laboratory Juanse made their own concoctions and medicines (nowadays it's a normal pharmacy). Colourful 19th- and early 20th-century tiled facades are a feature of the area and have been incorporated into the fronts of many modern shops and restaurants.

## Chueca

East of Calle de Fuencarral, bordered by Calle de Fernando VI, Calle Barquillo and Gran Vía, is the area of **Chueca**. After running the gamut from 19th-century affluence to 20th-century neglect, it has undergone a fashionable renaissance and is now Madrid's elegant reply to London's Soho.

Chueca's characterful narrow streets, with their mass of restaurants, bars, interior design shops, bookshops, arts and environmental businesses, run all the way to Gran Vía. Much of the business life and the buzzing street scene here is gay, and the mood is an open one which fills the *terrazas* on **Plaza** de Chueca **30**, winter and summer alike, with Madrid's most fashionable people watchers, local and international. Clubs and music bars also abound. Its Gay Pride Day (Día del Orgullo) in June is one of the summer's biggest events and the quarter's own annual fiesta.

On 17 January, animals ranging from pigs to pampered poodles queue with their owners outside the **Iglesia de San Antón** (open for mass only), Calle de Hortaleza, to be blessed by the priest. Inside, the church has a fine Goya painting and St Valentine's bones.

On the northern side of Chueca is the striking **Palacio de Longoria 31** (Calle Fernando VI 6), Madrid's only flamboyant Gaudí-style modernist building, designed as a private mansion by José Grases Riera in 1902, and today owned by the Spanish writers' and artists' copyright association (Sociedad General de Autores). Look up to the top of buildings around here and you will see fine Modernist details: lizards, penguins and other natural details. A few streets away, the **Museo Nacional de Romanticismo 32** (Calle San Mateo 13; Tue–Sat 9.30am–6.30pm, May–Oct until 8.30pm, Sun and hols 10am–3pm; www.museoromanticismo.es) transports you to a bourgeois city mansion in the time of Isabel II.

Pooches and their owner waiting to be blessed outside Iglesia de San Antón

## Plaza de España

As Gran Vía continues downhill towards the **Plaza de España** two 1950s skyscrapers, **Torre de Madrid** and **Edificio de España**, come into sight. When you reach the centre of the square you find the **Cervantes monument** where many pay homage to the great writer: a stone sculpture honouring him looms behind bronze statues of his immortal characters, Don Quixote and Sancho Panza, astride their horse and donkey, respectively.

**Calle de la Princesa**, which begins at Plaza de España, is actually a northwest extension of the Gran Vía. Tucked away in extensive grounds behind high railings, the neoclassical **Palacio de Liria** at No 22 is the residence of the Duchess of Alba. The renowned family art collection includes works by Rembrandt, Titian, Rubens, Van Dyck, El Greco and Goya, but it is only open to view on Fridays and by prior arrangement (tel: 91-547 5302).

## South of Princesa

On Calle Ventura Rodríguez at No. 17 is the **Museo Cerralbo** ㉝ (Tue–Sat 9.30am–3pm, Thur 5-8pm, Sun and hols

Torre de Madrid on Plaza de España

10am–3pm; charge; free Thur pm, Sat from 2pm, Sun; www.museocerralbo. mcu.es) gives insight into the lifestyle enjoyed by the Spanish nobility during the 19th century. Don Enrique de Aguilera y Gamboa, Marqués de Cerralbo (1845–1922), was a compulsive collector, traveller and scholar. His town house, built in 1883, was bequeathed to the

Templo de Debod

nation together with thousands of objets d'art. The artistic highlight is El Greco's *The Ecstasy of St Francis of Assisi* (in the chapel). No less impressive are works by Titian, Tintoretto and Alonso Cano in the Galería de Pintura and a fine collection of Spanish *bodegones*, or still lifes. Of all the many grand rooms, the ballroom is undoubtedly the finest.

Beyond the south side of the Plaza de España is **Parque del Oeste**, a green oasis where people come to enjoy the summer and autumn sunsets. It is home to the **Templo de Debod** ❸❹ (Tue–Fri Apr–Sept 10am–2pm and 6–8pm, Oct–Mar 9.45am–1.45pm and 4.15–6.15pm, Sat–Sun, hols and Aug, Tue–Sun 10am–2pm; free). The ancient Egyptian temple was given to the Spain as a gesture of thanks to the Spanish engineers involved in the Aswan Dam project.

## MONCLOA AND THE WEST

At the northern end of Calle de la Princesa is **Moncloa**, home to Madrid's Complutense University. Landmarks here date from Franco's dictatorship: the air force headquarters (inspired by El Escorial) and Madrid's youngest triumphal

arch, **Arco de la Victoria**, which commemorates the victory of General Franco's forces, when they took Madrid in 1939 after a two-year siege. Much of the area around it was destroyed during his approach.

The **Faro de Moncloa** is a 100-m (330-ft) high transmission mast which was built in 1990 complete with observation deck for panoramic views, but at the time of going to print, despite plans for reopening, is still closed to the public.

Just beyond Moncloa is the **Museo de América** ㉟ (Avenida de los Reyes Católicos 6, Ciudad Universitaria;

Goya's frescoes in the cupola of San Antonio de la Florida

Tue–Sat 9.30am–8.30pm; Sun and hols 10am–3pm; charge; www.museodeamerica.mcu. es). Its superb collection of art and artefacts from Central and South America includes the Madrid Codex, 56 pages of bark-paper leaves, one of only four surviving examples of the Maya people's writing, and two series of the famous colonial caste paintings. You need at least two hours to enjoy the museum's entire collection which is unique in Europe.

For aficionados of Spanish art, and Goya in particular, a visit to **La Ermita de San Antonio de la Florida** ㊱ (Glorieta de San Antonio de la Florida 5; Tue–Fri 9.30am–8pm, Sat–Sun and hols 10am–2pm; free) is a must. Goya's great frescoes, remarkably preserved, covering the cupola and walls of the

18th-century chapel, mark the emergence of his free, impressionistic style after the illness which left him deaf. The narrative piece in the cupola, capturing a street crowd, is regarded as one of his greatest achievements. The artist's tomb was installed in the church in 1919 and in 1929 an identical chapel was built alongside this one so Goya's frescoes and remains could rest undisturbed by worshippers.

Next to the chapel is **Casa Mingo**, one of Madrid's best loved terrace restaurants, and opposite you have access to the walking path along the city's small river, the **Río Manzanares**, which leads back to Principe Pío station and links up with Madrid Río, a vast landscaped riverbank area, with fountains and bridges, running down to the Puente de Segovia.

## Casa de Campo

To the west of the Río Manzanares is another former royal preserve, **Parque Casa de Campo**, forested by Felipe II in 1559. It can be reached by car, bus, suburban railway line, metro (Lago) or cable car (teleferico). The **cable car** (changing timetable; weekends only in winter; www.teleferico.com) takes you from the top of the Parque del Oeste across the river and into the heart of the park, an enormous heathland of pines, shrubs, gulleys and grassy slopes, where medieval monarchs hunted *jabalí* (wild boar). Among the pines beneath the cable car you can see traces of Civil War trenches from the city's three-year siege and you may see prostitutes blatantly touting their wares on the roads that cross the park (this is not a safe area at night).

Visitors can hire a boat on the lake (which has a huge spouting fountain), swim in open-air pools (June–Sept), or visit the **Zoo-Aquarium** (daily from 10.30am, with a changing timetable; charge; www.zoomadrid.com), where some 150 kinds of animal pace back and forth behind moats, not bars. There's also a funfair called the **Parque**

**de Atracciones** (daily, with a changing timetable; charge; www.parquedeattracciones.com).

# EXCURSIONS

One of Madrid's great advantages for visitors is its position as a central leap-off point to explore Castile. El Escorial, the Valle de los Caídos, Toledo, Segovia, Aranjuez, Chinchón and Ávila are all easy day trips from the capital and you can go much further afield in a day by AVE high-speed bullet trains. If you're travelling by car, note that heavy traffic jams are typical if you head out of the city on Friday night and back into Madrid from 5pm on Sunday, particularly in summer and on holiday weekends. A more relaxing option is to use public transport.

## El Escorial

A 40-minute drive from the centre of Madrid, or a one-hour train journey, takes you to **El Real Monasterio de San Lorenzo de El Escorial** ③ (Tue–Sun and hols, Oct–Mar 10am–6pm, Apr–Sept 10am–8pm; charge). El Escorial is the material realisation of the obsession of one man, Felipe II. A huge construction, built between 1563 and 1584, it takes its theme from a victory over the French in 1557 at St Quentin (now San Lorenzo's *fiesta* day), and incorporated the royal family's mausoleum. Felipe II, an introverted, deeply religious man, wanted a place in which he could retreat from his duties as king of the world's mightiest empire and be surrounded by monks, rather than courtiers, so El Escorial was designed as an austere royal residence, a library and a monastery for the Order of Hieronymites.

The enormous quadrilateral of granite stuck on to the flanks of the Sierra de Guadarrama is chillingly austere and vast: it has 86 staircases and more than 2,500 windows. Its

El Escorial

structure, with interlocking rectangles offset by spiky towers at the corners, was devised in the 16th century by Juan Bautista de Toledo and completed by Juan de Herrera.

Despite his reputation for gloomy fanaticism, Felipe II had an eye for art, and some of his best acquisitions have remained at El Escorial: canvases by Titian, Veronese and Tintoretto hang alongside works by Hieronymus Bosch and other masters from Flanders, which was then a Spanish territory. At the entrance to the Habsburg living quarters is El Greco's vast *Martyrdom of St Maurice*. Felipe II's lack of enthusiasm for this painting, now considered a masterpiece, led El Greco to settle in Toledo in search of Church patronage rather than royal commissions.

The suite of royal **living quarters** reflects Felipe's austere personal habits and piety. Everything is sparse in the study from which he ruled an empire and the attached bedroom has views of the basilica's altar.

In contrast, the richly decorated **Royal Pantheon**, located under the altar of the vast basilica, holds the remains of 23 kings and queens of Spain – the latter being admitted only if they had become the mother of a future sovereign. Felipe V, who loathed El Escorial, and Fernando VI are absent, by their own request. Alabaster tombs for surplus daughters, sons who never made it to the throne, and royal bastards are peripheral to the main vault, but prolific. The last royal figure to be laid to rest here was Juan de Borbón, who was obliged by General Franco to cede his rights to the throne in favour of his son, Spain's present King Juan Carlos I. Juan de Borbón died in Pamplona on 1 April 1993 and was interred two days later, earning his place as the son and father of kings, though he was never a king himself.

El Escorial's **library** is said to rank second only to the Vatican's in quality. The gilt edges of the books face outwards on the shelves to preserve the spines. Pope Gregory XII ordered

El Escorial's spectacular gilded library

the excommunication of anyone who stole a manuscript from here.

The town's tourist office (www.sanlorenzoturismo. org) is adjacent to the palace. Ask for a free map to find your way to the **Casita del Príncipe** (Casita de Abajo), set in a park below the palace, and to the **Casita del Infante** (Casita de Arriba), a shorter but more strenuous stroll uphill, following the Paseo de Carlos III. (Both may be visited during the

Valle de los Caídos monument

same hours as the main palace for an extra charge.) These late 18th century pleasure palaces were built for the sons of Carlos III and are furnished as opulently as any of Madrid's fully-fledged royal residences.

## Valle de los Caídos

Just around the mountain is another monument of enormous proportions, but far more polemical. After the Spanish Civil War, Franco wanted to build a monument to commemorate those who died during the hostilities. For the site he chose the V-shaped valley called Cuelgamuros known today as the **Valle de los Caídos** (Valley of the Fallen). The most visible part of the monument is a huge cross standing 150m (492ft) high, set upon the summit of a small mountain. Equally grand is the underground **Basilica** open to the public (Tue–Sun 10am– 6.30pm, until 6pm Oct–Mar; charge; www.valledeloscaidos. es). Carved 240m (786ft) deep into the granite mountain, using prisoner-of-war labour from the Republican forces,

Toledo's impressive Alcázar

the basilica is reached via a tunnel. The tombs of Franco and José Antonio Primo de Rivera, founder of the Falangist Party, occupy a privileged position, making this a place of homage for his followers. Ossuaries in the crypt (closed to the public) contain the remains of tens of thousands of the dead, of both sides, from the Civil War, making private reburial impossible, despite descendents' requests.

## Toledo

If you have just one day available for an excursion from Madrid, **Toledo** ⏱, the country's Visigothic capital in the 6th century, is a good choice. Originally a Roman fortress, it reached its zenith in the Muslim period and after the Christian Reconquest by Alfonso VI in the 11th century, when it became capital of Castile. Alfonso was crowned emperor of Spain and a two-century 'Golden Age' ensued. The court's transfer to Madrid in 1561 triggered the economic decline of the former capital. Nearly four centuries of stagnation ensured Toledo's preservation as one of the world's great medieval cities.

To enjoy Toledo's history and beauty at its best you need to work around the massive influx of tourists it receives on day excursions. Even Toledo's renowned steel craftsmen, whose traditional skills such as 'damascening' – cutting pigmented patterns in the metal – are rooted in the city's Moorish heritage, have had to take action against the producers of thousands of trashy items sold as souvenirs. So while the city may be seen in a day (a high-speed train from Atocha makes the journey in 35 minutes), the best way to avoid the crowds and enjoy the historic centre is to stay overnight (www.toledo-turismo.com).

A good place to start a visit is **Museo de Los Concilios y Cultura Visigoda Ⓐ** (Iglesia de San Roman; Tue–Sat 10am–2pm and 4–6.30pm, Sun 10am–10pm), which explores the city's Visigothic legacy. It is housed in the beautiful 13th-century *mudéjar* church of **San Roman**, which was probably built on the ruins of an earlier mosque, which in turn was built on the site of a Visigoth church. Such are the layers of Toledo's history.

Before the structure of the Church crystallised and Toledo's cathedral became the symbol of its power, there was a period of relative tolerance in the late Middle Ages when Islam, Christianity and Judaism coexisted quite comfortably. Their famed *convivencia*, as it is known, produced a cultural flowering expressed in medicine and the sciences, literature and translation, architecture and the arts. In particular, the *mudéjar* architecture and decoration created by Muslim craftsmen who stayed in Spain after the Reconquest reached a high point here between the 12th and 16th centuries. It was adopted by the Jewish community, too, after the onset of Christian persecution in the 14th century.

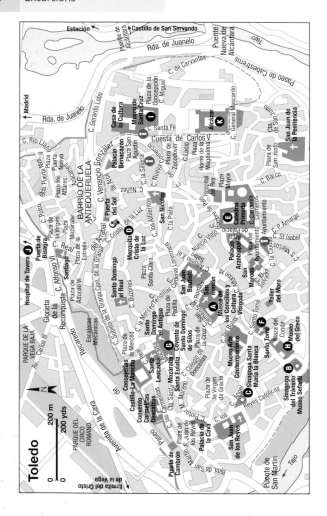

Toledo

Two historic synagogues stand on the southwestern slope of the city – the **Sinagoga del Tránsito**  (changing visitor hours), built for Pedro the Cruel's treasurer, Samuel Levi, in the second half of the 14th century and today containing the small Museo Sefardi; and the 13th-century **Sinagoga de Santa María la Blanca** ❸ (daily 10am–5.45pm, summer until 7pm). Both show strong Moorish influence in their design, with horseshoe arches, arabesques and glazed tiles. By contrast, all that remains of the Muslim past is the **Mezquita Cristo de la Luz** ❹, later converted into a church, above the Puerta del Sol; and the **Puerta de la Bisagra**, the main entry point for visitors coming from Madrid.

The **Catedral** ❺ (Mon–Sat 10am–6.30pm, Sun 2–6.30pm; charge) is one of Spain's most spectacular sights. It is visible from any part of town thanks to its Gothic tower topped by a spire ringed by spikes. Built between the 13th

Toledo's rooftops at dusk

Suit of armour in the
Army Museum

and 15th centuries, it is remarkable for its design, the carvings and paintings in its chapels and choir and later accumulated additions. It remains the first seat of the Primate of Spain. The Sacristy contains works by El Greco, Goya, Van Dyke and Bellini. Other highlights include the frescoed chapter house and the 16th-century stained glass in the transept.

El Greco's masterpiece, *The Burial of the Count of Orgaz*, is on display in the **Iglesia de Santo Tomé** Ⓕ, close to the cathedral (daily 10am–6pm, summer until 7pm; charge; www.santotome.org). The artist painted himself into the picture – he's the seventh figure from the left at the bottom, staring straight ahead. Earlier paintings in the **Convento de Santo Domingo de Silos** Ⓖ where he and his wife were buried – are also of interest. In this area, too, stands the **Museo del Greco** Ⓗ (Po del Transito; Tue–Sat 9.30am–8pm, Oct–Mar until 6.30pm; Sun and hols 10am–3pm; charge, free Sat from 4pm and Sun; www.museodelgreco).

Near the **Plaza de Zocodover**, in the heart of Toledo, is the **Museo de Santa Cruz** Ⓘ (Mon–Sat 10am–7pm, Sun 10am–2.30pm; free), a fine Renaissance building displaying more works by El Greco, Ribera and Goya.

Beyond the city walls, in the northern district of Las Covachuela, the **Hospital de Tavera** Ⓙ (Mon–Sat 10am–1.30pm and 3–5.30pm, Sun and hols 10am–1.30pm;

charge) exhibits works by El Greco, Tintoretto, Titian, Zur-barán and Ribera.

Dominating the city is the enormous **Alcázar** Ⓚ (Thur–Tue 11am–5pm; charge, free on Sun), a fortress destroyed and rebuilt many times since the Roman era. The latest destruction occurred during the Civil War. The fortress now houses a five-storey **Army Museum** with displays relating to the dramatic 72-day siege.

Travelling to Toledo by train will enable you to admire its grand neo-*mudéjar* **railway station**, built for Alfonso XIII's visits to the city. In the 1920s, this was the starting point for evenings of the Grand Order of Toledo, a group of surreal-ists, including Salvador Dalí and Luis Buñuel, who met with the sole object of drinking the night away in good company in Toledo.

If you're driving back to Madrid from Toledo and want to make a brief stop, the village of **Illescas** (33km/20 miles from Toledo) keeps five paintings by El Greco, which hang in the church of the local Hospital de la Virgen de la Caridad (Convent of the Virgin of Charity).

## El Greco in Toledo

El Greco spent the most productive years of his prolific career in Toledo. Just down the hill from Santo Tomé, the Museo del Greco – misleadingly named, since the artist almost certainly never lived in it – has been reconstructed and linked to a museum dedicated to his life. Still, it has authentic 16th-century furnishings and a tranquil garden that replicate the look and feel of a Toledan house of the era. Several of the master's paintings are on display, among them A *View of Toledo* and *Portrait of St Peter*. The El Greco house was originally built by Samuel Levi, a 14th-century Jewish financier and friend of King Pedro the Cruel of Castile.

## Segovia

Located 88km (55 miles) northwest of Madrid, now easily reached by AVE high-speed train (45 minutes and frequent buses or taxis) **Segovia ③⑨** rises majestically from the surrounding plains. The city's setting is picturesque *campo* – wide-open plains interrupted by an occasional monastery or castle – with the slopes of the Sierra de Guadarrama filling half the horizon.

Segovia is a city of great monuments, all testament to epochs of glory: a 2,000-year-old aqueduct, a fine cathedral and a later storybook alcázar. It also has dozens of smaller churches, cultural sites and experiences that may be visited seasonally (www.turismodesegovia.com)

The wondrous **Roman Aqueduct Ⓐ**, a work of art and a triumph of engineering, marches right across the entrance of the town. The aqueduct is composed of thousands of granite blocks arranged in graceful arches, sometimes two-tiered, but without mortar or cement. It is nearly 1km (0.5 miles) long, and it rises to a height of 46m (150ft). This is the last lap of a conduit that brought water from a mountain stream to the walled city. The aqueduct was in constant use for 100 generations, with only a couple of details changed. In the 16th century, a statue of Hercules in a niche over the tallest arch was replaced by a Christian image.

The **Alcázar Ⓑ**, Segovia's fairytale royal castle (daily 10am–6pm, until 7pm Apr–Sept; charge; www.alcazardesegovia.com), was erected on a ridge overlooking the confluence of two rivers, with an unimpeded view of the plateau in all directions. The Romans are thought to have built a watchtower here. The present castle, reportedly the model for the first Disneyland, is a far cry from the simple stone fortress that took shape in the 12th century. As the fortress grew bigger and more luxurious, it also came to play a significant historical role. By the 13th century, parliaments were convened here. The most fanciful and photogenic parts of the castle's superstructure – its feast of turrets and towers – are the work of restoration after a disastrous fire in 1862. A hefty climb up the tower will be rewarded by breathtaking views of Segovia and the valley beyond.

From whatever part of town you view it, the **Catedral**  (daily 9.30am–5.30pm, Sun until 1pm or 1.30pm, summer until 6.30pm; charge) is a beautiful sight. Its pinnacles, buttresses and cupolas seem to belong to a whole complex of churches. Begun in 1525 (but not consecrated until 1768), this is the last of the great Spanish Gothic cathedrals.

Segovia's Roman aqueduct

Incidentally, the cathedral was even taller before a lightning bolt lopped off the main tower in 1614. The reconstruction plan warily lowered the profile by more than 10 percent.

Inside, the cathedral's majestic columns and arches are lit by fine stained-glass windows. Two 18th-century organs are spectacularly flamboyant. Less obvious are the altarpieces in the chapels, the most important element of which is a 16th-century polychrome *Pietà* by the Valencian Juan de Juan, just to the right of the entrance.

Delicate arches line the cloister, which belonged to a former cathedral that was destroyed and was moved here, stone by stone, in the 16th century. The adjacent museum and chapter

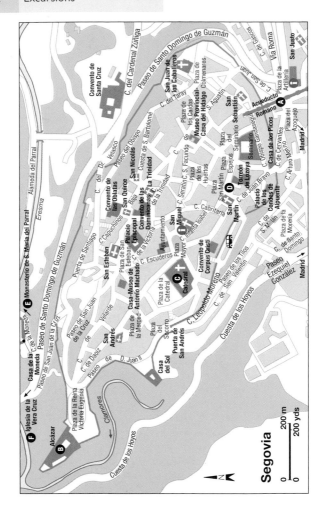

Segovia

house contain a number of interesting pieces of religious art and relics, including 17th-century tapestries, the Baroque carriage propelled through the streets of Segovia every Corpus Christi (in June), and the reminder of a 14th-century tragedy: the tomb of the infant Prince Pedro, son of Enrique II. He slipped from the arms of his nurse as she admired the

Segovia's Alcázar

view from an open window of the Alcázar. Legend has it she scarcely hesitated before she leaped after him to her death in the moat below.

Segovia's main square, the **Plaza Mayor**, combines history with real-life bustle. The 17th-century town hall faces the large oblong plaza where shoppers, businessmen and tourists take time out for coffee in the fresh air.

A few streets away to the east, a church much older than the cathedral graces Segovia's loveliest square. La Iglesia de San Martín is a 12th-century Romanesque beauty with glorious portals and porches (open for mass only). **Plaza de San Martín D**, which slopes down to Calle de Juan Bravo, is surrounded by noble mansions. Next to the church, the building with stark, barred windows was built as a prison in the 17th century; it now houses a library. Here and throughout the city, the facades of buildings are subject to elaborate three-dimensional decoration, mainly with geometric forms. The most unusual example, the nearby Casa de los Picos, bristles with pointed protuberances.

Total tranquillity permeates the **Monasterio de El Parral E** (Tue–Sat 10am–12.30pm, Sun and hols until 11.30am,

Segovia's skyline

and daily 4.15–6.30pm; voluntary charge), founded in the mid-15th century just beyond the city walls but within easy reach of the centre of town. The architectural details, including a Gothic cloister, are being restored in fits and starts. After a Sunday morning visit, you can hear a sung Mass, with Gregorian chant.

Also just outside the wall and almost in the shadow of the Alcázar, is the stunning **Iglesia de la Vera Cruz** **F** (Tue–Sun 10.30am–1.30pm and 4–6pm, summer until 7pm; charge), a 12-sided structure dating from the early 13th century. The knights of the Holy Sepulchre held court in its unique double-decker chapel, surrounded by a circular nave.

## Aranjuez

A 40-minute journey south of Madrid by train or bus lies **Aranjuez** **40** (www.aranjuez.es) its setting beside the River Tagus highlighted by its splendid Royal Palace. The **Real**

**Palacio de Aranjuez** (daily 10am–6pm, Apr–Sept until 8pm; charge), was built by Felipe II and rebuilt during the reign of Fernando VI after a fire in 1748 destroyed most of the interior but left the original 16th-century structure intact. Carlos IV and his queen, María Luisa, furnished it to the hilt. Here you will see a porcelain-lined room even more elaborate than the one in Madrid's Royal Palace. Goya's portrait of Fernando VII shows him for the brutish dictator he turned out to be. The chandeliers are particularly fine. One of the studies is filled with 203 framed watercolour sketches that make for an illustrated encyclopedia of life in China during the mid-19th century, with customs, trades, temples, flora and fauna meticulously depicted. These were a gift from the Emperor of China to Isabel II. During her reign, too, the smoking room was decorated in layers of stucco to reproduce the Tower of the Two Sisters at the Alhambra, with the red, green and gold colours that have faded from the original.

But in many respects, the Palace of Aranjuez is outdone by its satellite, the **Casita del Labrador** (Worker's Cottage), a rococo-style pavilion built for Carlos IV in response to the Petit Trianon at Versailles. Situated at the far end of the royal gardens, it is packed with 18th-century bric-à-brac.

Aranjuez is equally visited for its parks and gardens. The most beautiful are the 18th-century Jardín de la Isla and Jardín del Principe (Garden Island and Prince's Garden; daily 8am–9pm, winter until 6.30pm). A small museum here, which is known as the Casa de Marinos or Museo de

### Strawberry train

On summer weekends you can travel from Madrid to Aranjuez by a special train, the Tren de las Fresas, on which strawberries (fresas) are handed out by girls wearing traditional costumes. Tickets cost about €30 (www.museodelferro carril.org).

Falúas (Museum of Ceremonial Barges), displays decorative boats used for royal river trips.

## Chinchón

The picture-postcard town of **Chinchón** ④ 52km (32 miles) south of Madrid and a 10-minute bus or car ride east of Aranjuez, remains surprisingly rural. It is famous for its historic **Plaza Mayor**, used for bullfights since at least 1502 and as the setting for a renowned Passion Play on the evening of Easter Saturday. Surrounded by three-storey wooden galleries, the *plaza* is both rustic and elegant.

Chinchón (www.ciudadchinchon.com) is famous for its bars in which you can try the local aniseed-based tipple, *anís*, and restaurants serving charcoal-grilled *chorizo* and meat, which may be cooked with the excellent local garlic, another speciality.

## Ávila

From Madrid, road and rail routes climb through spectacular woodlands, streams and rugged peaks to reach Ávila province, a wild tundra-like plateau dotted with wind-eroded shrubs and huge boulders. This austere landscape – a source of inspiration for St Teresa and other mystics – is one of the highest inhabited areas in Spain.

Its provincial capital, located approximately 100km (60 miles) north-west of Madrid, is the medieval walled city of **Ávila** ④ (www.avilaturismo.com).

### Musical inspiration

The most popular guitar concerto ever, Joaquín Rodrigo's *Concierto de Aranjuez*, was inspired by the beautiful river gardens at the Palacio Real. The music transports the listener to the palace surrounded by nature; Rodrigo described it as 'capturing the fragrance of magnolias, the singing of birds and the gushing of fountains'.

Ávila is the highest provincial capital in Spain so until as late as April it can be bitterly cold up there. The **Muralla**, or city wall – over 2km (1.2 miles) long and with no less than 88 watchtowers and nine gates – is the best preserved in Europe. It may be climbed via two points of access, El Alcázar and Las Carnicerías (Tue–Sun 11am– 6pm, Apr–Sept 10am–8pm; charge). The apse of the **Catedral** (Mon–Fri 10am–5pm, Sat until 6pm, Sun and hols noon–5pm, 1 hour more in summer; charge) sticks out to form a part of these fortifications. The city has been a magnet for pilgrims

The medieval walls of Ávila

ever since the late 16th century, as the birthplace of St Teresa, the great reformer of the Carmelite Order. Visitors can see Teresa's birthplace, now marked by a 17th-century church; the convent where she lived much of her life, the Monasterio de Encarnación; and the Convento de San José, the first she founded in the city.

Other notable sights include the **Basílica de San Vicente**, built on the site where San Vicente and his two sisters were martyred in the 4th century; and the 15th-century Monasterio de Santo Tomé, with its three haunting cloisters and marble tomb of Fernando and Isabel's only son, Don Juan, who died aged 19.

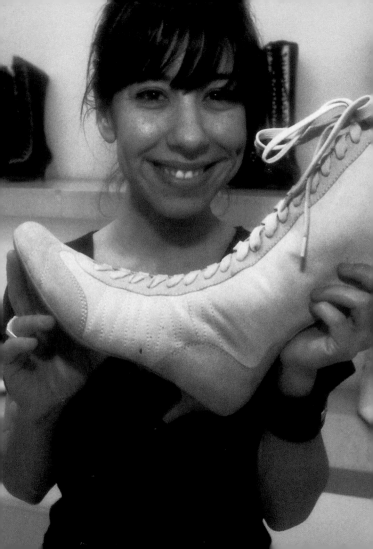

# WHAT TO DO

## SHOPPING

Madrid's major department stores are located in the centre between the Puerta del Sol and Callao, and along the Gran Vía. More select designers line Calle de Serrano and its adjoining streets in Salamanca. Calle del Prado, La Latina and Puerta de Toledo are good for antiques. For high-street shops try Calle del Arenal, Sol, Calle de Preciados, Gran Vía and Calle de la Princesa. Calle de Fuencarral is the city's main drag for hip young fashion from home and abroad, with more expensive one-off designs in Chueca in newer alternative shops scattered through Malasaña and its subzone Triball.

Madrid's major department-store chain is El Corte Inglés (branches at Calle de Serrano 47; Calle de Preciados 3; Calle de la Princesa 41; Calle de Goya 76, on the corner of Calle del Alcalá; and Calle Raimundo Fernández Villaverde 1). Note that department stores often offer a 10 percent discount to foreign shoppers (ask in the store for details).

Among Madrid's central shopping centres **La Vaguada** (Avenida Monforte de Lemos s/n, Barrio del Pilar), in northern Madrid, is a multi-level complex with 300 bars, restaurants and cinemas. **ABC Serrano** (Calle de Serrano 61) is the most central mall, but smaller, with selected stylish shops, café and restaurant.

Only shopping centres and department stores are guaranteed to stay open through the day. Opening hours are generally Monday–Friday, 9 or 10am until 1.30pm or 2pm, and 4pm or 5pm until 8pm. On Saturday, stores tend to open from 9.30am until 1.30pm. Sunday opening has taken off in the

Spanish leather boots are a good buy

city centre, particularly around Puerta del Sol, but is not yet general through the city.

## What to Buy

There's no shortage of items to take home, from traditional Spanish fans to foodstuffs or cutting edge fashions.

**Books:** There's an outdoor second-hand book stand open daily on Pasadizo de San Ginés, off Calle del Arenal, and on Cuesta de Moyano, near Atocha, at weekends. From late May, a book fair takes over the Retiro for several weeks. Antonio Machado (Marqués de Casa Riera 2 and Fernando VI 17) is a good Spanish bookshop. El Central de Callao, Postigo de San Martín 8, open daily 10am–10pm, stocks gifts, cards and magazines as well as a huge array of carefully stocked books.

**Crafts:** The streets below Plaza Mayor have unusual craft shops. Casa Hernanz (Calle Toledo 18), specialises in espadrilles

---

### The Rastro

On Sunday morning Madrid's most famous street market, the Rastro, selling everything from antiques, books and fashions to pets and coal-burning stoves, spreads through Lavapiés from Tirso de Molina to Ronda de Embajadores. A good starting point for exploring the quarter is the Plaza del Cascorro, while further down the Ribera de Curtidores – the market's main avenue – is the rastro itself, the slaughterhouse after which the market is named.

Some of the most interesting finds are on and around the Plaza General Vara del Rey, where antiques stalls and shops sell second-hand cameras, books and postcards. If you seriously want to buy, arrive by 9.30am. By midday the streets are packed. Be on the alert for pickpockets – this is unfortunately a notorious place for thieving.

Leave time for a tapa in one of the busy bars. The Rastro starts to pack up at about 3pm.

(*alpargatas*), Cerería Ortega (Calle Toledo 43) in candles and the Corchera Castellana (Cava Baja 47) in cork items.

**Antiques**: Head to the Rastro. In nearby streets are more solid establishments dealing in old objets d'art. Centro de Arte y Antiguedades (Calle de Serrano 5) has multiple dealers under a single roof, some with very fine and unusual items.

**Fashion**: Spanish fashion has produced major brands and designers in the last three decades. For the big couture names, head for Salamanca – on Calle de Serrano, look for Hoss Intropia (No. 18), Loewe Mujer (No. 26), and

Fans for keeping cool

Hombre (No. 34). For high street and budget fashion, explore Calle de Fuencarral. Zara – the largest branch, with two shop spaces, is at Gran Vía 52–54. Custo and Camper (Fuencarral 29 and 42) are key brands

**Flamenco**: Music, clothes and instruments are found at El Flamenco Vive (Conde de Lemos 7), close to Opera.

**Food and Drink**: Lavinia (Calle José Ortega y Gasset 16) stocks over 2,000 Spanish wines, including Sherry (*jerez*), and Rioja and Ribera del Duero red and white *crianzas, reservas and gran reservas*. The municipal markets are an unmissable experience for food lovers (Anton Martín in Lavapiés and La Paz in Salamanca are good examples). The gourmet food departments of El Corte Inglés have a good range too.

Bars spill onto the streets near Plaza Mayor

**Leather:** Salvador Bachiller (Gran Vía 65 and three other branches) makes stunning bags, suitcases, wallets and other items in a huge range of colours.

# ENTERTAINMENT

## Nightlife

Madrid nightlife is hectic, fast-moving and carries on all night. In the early 1980s, *la movida*, the arts and nightlife nurtured by the socialist mayor, Enrique Tierno Galván, created such a sense of street fiesta that exhausted people would sigh, *Madrid me mata* – Madrid is killing me. Constantly in search of the ultimate in *marcha*, or fun, young Madrileños flock into the city centre after work, usually from Thursday to Saturday and at least until sunrise.

Good starting points for an evening stroll are the *cervecerías* on the Plaza Santa Ana (sedate), the central boulevard of the

Paseo del Prado (smart), or the tascas and *tavernas* in Huertas (young), where you can have a bite to eat before things get going in the clubs, bars and discos. In Malasaña, Plaza Dos de Mayo is peppered with alternative bars; while Chueca, to the north of the Gran Vía, the vibrant centre of Madrid's gay scene, is the hip equivalent of New York's SoHo, with dozens of gay and hetero bars, clubs and restaurants.

Madrid nightlife provides a wealth of cultural experiences. Our top choices are listed below:

**Live Music Clubs.** There are plenty of places in Madrid for live jazz and Latin music. **Café Central** (Plaza del Ángel 10) is a long-standing jazz café near Plaza de Santa Ana, with nightly music. **Populart** (Calle de las Huertas 22) has a more wide-ranging line-up including jazz, reggae and blues. **Clamores** (Albuquerque, 14) also has interesting, eclectic programming.

Café Central in full swing

**After-Hours Clubs.** Venues, the sessions they host and prices change all the time. Here are a sampling of highlights between Wednesday and Sunday nights: **Bash** Plaza del Callao 4, funky, hip-hop, R&B (Wed midnight–6am); **Mockba**, in Changó Covarrubias 42, electronic (Fri midnight–6am); **The Room**, in Shangai Club, Cost de los Ángeles, 20, electro (Sat midnight–6am); **Space of Sound**

**What's on**

To find out what is on, consult the magazine *Guía del Ocio* (www.guiadelocio. com), out every Friday and available from kiosks.

in Macumba, Pl de Chamartín s/n, considered one of Spain's best sessions, changing DJs, everything from underground house to deep and tribal (Sun noon–midnight, current entry cost €15–20).

## Music and Theatre

**Classical Music, Opera and Dance**. As home to the National Orchestra, the Spanish Radio and Television Symphony, the Compania Nacional de Danza (contemporary), the Ballet Nacional de España, and the city's and region's orchestras and dance companies, Madrid has an exceptional calendar of concerts, recitals and dance events.

Madrid's opera house, the **Teatro Real**, features big-name productions (Plaza Isabel II; www.teatro-real.com).

The **Auditorio Nacional de Música** (Príncipe de Vergara 146; www.auditorioncional.mcu.es) has excellent seasons of

## Flamenco

Spain's most unique art form is flamenco, built around its song, guitars, and – perhaps best known – its dance with percussive heels. Pure flamenco, which has grown around *cante jondo* (deep song) deals with human dramas of poverty, love and death in a slow, piercing manner. You can watch flamenco in clubs across the capital, including: **Café de Chinitas** (Calle Torija 7; www.chinitas.com; Metro: Santo Domingo); **Corral de la Morería** (Calle de la Morería 7; www.corraldelamoreria. com; Metro: Opera); **Casa Patas** (Calle Cañizares 10; www.casapatas. com; Metro: Antón Martín), a restaurant-bar with flamenco shows in a back room (Mon–Thur at 10.30pm, Fri and Sat at midnight and 2am) and **Las Tablas** (Pl de España; www.lastablasmadrid.com) which offers a more modern setting than traditional flamenco shows. However, many of the best performances are given in theatres and concert halls – check the newspaper for dates.

recitals and concerts, including experimental contemporary music and flamenco, throughout the year.

The **Teatro Lírico Nacional de la Zarzuela** (Calle de Jovellanos 4; www.teatrodelazarzuela.mcu.es) and **Teatros del Canal** (Calle Cea Bermúdez 1; www.teatroscanal.com) are Madrid's main contemporary, classical and world dance venues.

**Theatre**. Spain's dramatic tradition is long and glorious. In dozens of Madrid theatres, classical and contemporary foreign and Spanish works are performed. Among those with the greatest critical acclaim are the following: **Teatro de Abádia** (Calle Fernández de

Flamenco dancers, or *bailaora*, in action.

los Ríos 42; www.teatroabadia.com), at the former Church of La Sagrada Familia, offers quality contemporary drama. **Teatro de la Comedia** (Calle del Príncipe 14; currently closed for restoration) puts on classic Spanish works, by playwrights such as Federico García Lorca and Lope de Vega. **Teatro Español** (Calle del Príncipe 25; www.teatroespanol.es) and its new warehouse space, the **Matadero**, set the pace for excellent classic and contemporary international and home-grown theatre.

**Cinema**. Details of subtitled films shown in their original language (*version original* or *VO*) are published in the weekly Guía del Ocio and in daily papers such as *El País* and in *El Mundo's* Friday magazine *Metropoli*. The main cluster of VO cinemas, totalling 18 screens in all, is on Martín de los Heros and Princesa (Cines Yelmo, Princesa, Renoir Plaza de España and Renar Princesa).

**Teletickets**. Most theatre, dance, opera and some cinema tickets can be bought on the web. Try www.entradas.com, www.elcorteingles.es, www.catalunyacaixa.com.

## SPORTS

**Basketball**. Games are held in the Real Madrid Baloncesto installations, north of the Plaza de Castilla, or in the Palacio de Deportes on Avenida Felipe II. Two teams at the top of the Spanish league are Adecco Estudiantes and Real Madrid.

**Fútbol** (football/soccer). The world's number one sport is a passion in Spain. The two big Madrid teams are **Real Madrid** and **Atlético Madrid**. Tickets for Real Madrid matches can be obtained daily 6–9 pm from their central stadium: Estadio Santiago Bernabéu, Avenida de Concha Espina, by Tower A (Metro: Santiago Bernabéu; tel: 902-324 324; www.realmadrid. es). Tickets for Atlético Madrid can be obtained daily 11am–2pm and 5–8pm, as well as on match days from 11am to kick-off at their stadium in the southerly area of Piramides beside the River Manzanares: Estadio Vicente Calderón, Po Virgen del Puerto 67 (Metro: Piramides); tel: 902-260 403; www.club atleticomadrid.com.

**Golf**. There are 22 golf courses in the Madrid area. Greens are open to non-members on payment of a substantial greens fee. Contact the Real Federación Española de Golf, Capitán Haya 9, 28020 Madrid; www.rfegolf.es.

**Skiing**. From December to April, the Guadarrama mountains north of Madrid become a ski area. The scenery and facilities are first-rate, and all equipment may be hired. The most highly developed resort, with five ski-chairs and six ski-lifts, is Navacerrada, only 52km (32 miles) from Madrid, along the N6012. Expect the slopes to be packed when there is snow. **Valdesquí**, reached via the N1 and N601, 150km (92 miles) from Madrid, has six ski-lifts, a ski-school and a ski-tow. For more details see www.esquiespana.org.

Elsewhere in Madrid, various sports facilities cater to many interests. You'll find tennis courts, polo grounds, squash courts, swimming pools and riding stables.

## CHILDREN'S MADRID

The **Casa de Campo**, with its teleférico (cable car), funfair (Parque de Atracciones, see page 69), lake and open-air swimming is a good option on hot days. Also within the Casa de Campo, there's the **Madrid ZooAquarium**. The year-round circus at Circo Price, (Rda de Toledo 35; www.teatrocircoprice.es) is a reliable choice too.

Valdesquí ski resort

Attractions in the **Parque del Buen Retiro** include marionette shows at noon on Sundays and rowing on the lake (see page 52).

At **Safari Madrid** (Aldea del Fresno, National Highway V, near Navalcarnero; daily 10.30am–5.30pm; www.safarimadrid. com), elephants, rhinos, lions and zebra roam freely, and you can also get close up to birds of prey, insects and reptiles.

Closer to the city is **Faunia** (Avenida de la Comunidades 28, Metro: Valdebernardo; see website www.faunia.es for changing times throughout the year), a hugely successful new theme park simulating a variety of ecosystems and their fauna.

**Aquopolis** (Avenida de la Dehesa, Villanueva de la Cañada; mid-June–Sept; tel: 91-815 6911; www.aquapolis.com) is a large waterpark with wave pools, shoots, cascades and toddlers' pools. Free buses go from the city centre; check the website for details.

Other attractions include the **IMAX** cinema at Parque Tierno Galván (C Meneses s/n; www.imaxmadrid.com; Metro: Méndez Álvaro); the **Cosmocaixa Science Museum** (Alcobendas district; tel: 91-484 5200; Tue–Sun 10am–8pm; buses from the Plaza de Castilla), a great place for kids to learn about natural history, chemistry and the basic laws of physics; and the **Planetario de Madrid** (Planetarium; Parque Tierno Galván; Metro: Méndez Álvaro; tel: 91-467 3898; www.planet madrid.es), where shows start at 5pm and 6.45pm Tue–Fri and 11.30am, 12.45pm, 5.30pm and 6.45pm at weekends and holidays. **Imaginarium** (Claudio Cuello, 35 and other branches) is an exceptionally creative toyshop (www.imaginarium.com).

Located halfway between Madrid and Aranjuez, at San Martín de la Vega, **Parque Warner Madrid** (Ctra M301 km 15.5, tel: 902-024 100; www.parquewarner.com) offers five themed areas incorporating sets and characters from Warner Brothers films and cartoons. Among the attractions is an 80km/h (50mph) roller-coaster.

# Calendar of Events

As you plan your excursions, it is worth checking additional details of festivals and fairs with tourist information offices.

**January** *Día de los Reyes* (Three Kings Cavalcade). Procession through streets commemorating kings' pilgrimage to meet baby Jesus. San Anton. Blessing of pets and animals at San Anton church, Calle Haraleza.

**February** *Carnaval.* Week before Lent celebrated with the Entierro de la Sardina (Burial of the Sardine) on Paseo de la Florida. ARCO (Contemporary Art Fair). Spain's largest international art fair, usually the second week in February.

**March/April** Semana Santa (Holy Week). Every town and city has striking processions. In cities with famous cathedrals, such as Toledo and Segovia, the spectacle is unforgettable. The town of Cuenca, 165km (100 miles) southeast of Madrid, is noted for its splendid processions.

**May** *Madrid: Fiestas de San Isidro* (St Isidore the Husbandman), the capital's patron saint. Half a month of neighbourhood parties, plays, concerts and daily bullfights.

**June Toledo**: *Corpus Christi.* The Spanish primate leads a solemn religious procession through the medieval streets. *Toledo Province: Camuñas.* An ancient religious play is presented in mime, with spectacular costumes. *Fiestas de San Juan* and *San Pedro.* Dances, bullfights, fireworks.

**July** *Ávila.* Outdoor festival with poetry, art, theatre, sports and bullfights.

**July–August** *Madrid: Veranus de la Villa.* Open-air festival of music and dance in central Madrid venues.

**August** *Madrid: Castizo* fiestas, the traditional fiestas of San Caeyetano, San Lorenzo and La Virgen de la Paloma, with much of the activity taking place around the Plaza de la Paja and the Jardines de las Vistillas. 15 August is a major national holiday and many towns have local celebrations.

**October–November** *Festival de Otoño.* The city's biggest cultural festival includes international theatre, jazz, dance and a host of other events.

**December** *Nochevieja* (New Year's Eve). Celebration in Madrid's Puerta del Sol; grapes are swallowed between each chime of the clock.

# EATING OUT

Madrid is a food lover's city: its restaurants are for those with every kind of budget and you can sample Spain's regional cuisine from around the country and world cuisine from Latin America to Asia. Apart from this, you cannot miss the city's take on the *tapeo*, the tapas crawl. Regional cuisine varies greatly, but Spanish cooking is never overly spicy; however, it is garlicky and liberally salted.

## Mealtimes

For many visitors, eating hours in Spain take some getting used to. Madrileños eat lunch and dinner late by most standards. Lunch usually isn't begun until 2 or 3pm and friends often meet for dinner at 9.30–10pm. Outside local hours

A plate of gambas

you are likely to find yourself dining alone. Swing into local habits and pace yourself, Spanish style, by grazing on tapas at your normal dinner time.

## Restaurants and Menus

Spaniards traditionally eat three courses at both lunch and dinner. However, it's not uncommon to share a first course, or to order *un sólo plato* (just a main course), if you're not that hungry. Many restaurants offer bargain

Waiter on Plaza Mayor

lunchtime set menus called the *menú del día*. For a fixed price (usually €8–14 in an everyday eatery, and €25–40 in a gourmet restaurant), you'll get a choice of first course, a main dish and dessert or coffee, plus a glass of either wine (or more), beer or bottled water, and bread.

Restaurants feature a grading system, from five forks to one, marked on the door of the restaurant. The system is an indication of price, and grades the facilities and service, not the quality of the food.

While restaurants offer a full menu, often with a fixed-price menu available, cafeterías usually focus on *platos combinados*, which combine main courses and accompaniments such as steak, eggs, chips and salad served on the same plate.

Most bars and *cervecerías* (draft beer bars) also serve tapas, sandwiches *(bocadillos)* or limited *platos combinados*. In summer their pavement terraces will look alluring, but remember, prices are higher if you sit at a table or outside rather than at the bar.

Enjoying *chocolate con churros*

The most insignificant meal of the day in Spain is generally breakfast, except at hotels, which offer continental breakfasts or buffets. A true Madrid breakfast is churros, fritters, sometimes made before your eyes. You can dunk churros in your coffee, or eat them as Spaniards do, with extremely thick, strong hot chocolate.

## Castilian Specialities

*Cocido madrileño* is one of many regional variations of the originally medieval, possibly Jewish one-pot stew found all over Spain. The meal often starts with *sopa de cocido*, the broth resulting from boiling the ingredients for the next course, before moving to the *cocido* itself: beef, cured ham, sausage, chickpeas, cabbage, onion and potatoes.

Another speciality is Castilian soup, also known as *sopa de ajo* or garlic soup. At the last moment, a raw egg is added to the soup, and by the time it reaches the table, the egg is well poached.

*Callos a la madrileña* is stewed tripe – try it if you like spicy-hot tomato sauce. For a lighter speciality, try *besugo al horno*, baked sea bream, once a Christmas dish.

Modern times have seen feasting dishes such as wood-roasted *cochinillo*, tender suckling pig, or *cordero*, roast lamb (often on the bone) become everyday specialities. Likewise *jamón serrano* or *Iberico*, thinly sliced cured ham, is a favourite *tapa*.

## Regional Specialities

Madrid has many restaurants specialising in food from the regions. Here are some dishes to look out for on menus of all kinds. Andalucía's most famous speciality is *gazpacho*, a chilled garlicky raw tomato soup to which chopped garnishes and croutons are added to taste. It's extremely refreshing on hot summer days and has inspired many modern avant-garde variants.

From Valencia comes one of Spain's great dishes. Paella is named after the flat metal pan in which rice is cooked with either meat or fish – traditionally not both together – plus garlic, saffron and peppers. Spaniards think of paella, and other rice dishes (*arroces*) as lunchtime dishes.

### Chocolate con Churros

It is a Madrileño custom to finish a late night with *chocolate con churros* (hot chocolate with deep-fried loops of batter). Try the following establishments:

**Chocolatería San Ginés,** Pzo San Ginés 7; daily 9.30am–7pm

**Chocolatería Muñiz,** Calle de Calatrava 3; daily 6.30–11am

**Chocolatería San Miguel,** Conde de Miranda 4; daily 7.30am–4pm, 6–9.30pm

**El Churro de Oro Escosura,** Calle Oro Escosura 13; daily 7am–10.30pm

The fine art of cutting *jamón*; the expensive ham is sliced by hand rather than with a meat slicer

*Fabada*, from Asturias, is a variation on Madrid's *cocido*, but is cooked with velvety white faba beans and regional charcuterie like black sausage and chorizo. *Trucha a la navarra*, grilled trout stuffed with a slice of ham, is a speciality of Navarra, while from Galicia there's *caldo gallego*, a rich vegetable soup.

A wide variety of sophisticated fish dishes come from the Basque country. Try *bacalao al pil pil* (salt cod in hot garlic sauce), *merluza a la vasca* (hake in a casserole with a thick sauce) or an extravagant luxury, *angulas a la bilbaína* (eels in a spicy olive oil and garlic sauce).

## Drinks
Wine menus today generally offer bottles from many Spanish denominations of origin: La Rioja, Navarra, Ribera del Duero, Jumilla, Somontano and Madrid are among the most popular.

Also try cava, sparkling wine from Catalonia – Spain's answer to champagne.

If you just say *tinto* (red) or *blanco* (white) when asked for your choice of *vino*, you'll be given the house wine, which may come in a glass, bottle or be decanted into a jug. Many Spanish diners use a little sparkling mineral water or lemonade (*casera*) to dilute wine, especially in summer.

Spanish beers, in bottles or on draught (*caña*), are generally light and refreshing. Sangría is prepared in some Madrid bars and all will prepare clara, a beer and lemonade shandy. Sherry (*Jerez*) from Jerez de la Frontera in Andalucia, is delicious when well kept. Pale dry fino is drunk chilled as an apéritif and also with soup and fish courses, while the rich, dark oloroso or PX is a good digestif. Spanish brandy varies: you get what you pay for. Other spirits, made under licence in Spain, are often cheaper than imported labelled spirits and served very generously.

Coffee is served black (*solo*), with a spot of milk (*cortado*), with hot milk (*con leche*) or with hot water (*americano*).

## Opening Hours, Payment and Prices

Note that a large number of restaurants close for at least one day a week, often Sunday evening and all day Monday. Old-fashioned and family businesses also close for some or all of August and currently many bars close between lunch and dinner.

For payment, you may need cash: many places do not accept all credit cards and some do not accept any.

Water and wine

Remember that for tapas, as well as meals, you generally pay at the end.

Curiously, Michelin-starred eating offers some of the best value if you look at set menu prices, which may be half of those in northern European capitals.

## Tapas and el Tapeo

Tapas – the small snacks for which Spanish bars and cafés are renowned – are one of Spain's great contributions to world cuisine.

The list of tapas is almost endless, but some of the more common are *aceitunas* (olives), *chorizo* (cured sausage), *champiñones* (mushrooms, usually fried in garlic), *queso* (cheese), *albóndigas* (meat balls), *croquetas* (croquettes of fish or chicken), *morcilla* (blood sausage), and the classic *tortilla española*, an omelette with potatoes fried in olive oil until golden.

A small plate is called a *tapa*, a larger serving, meant to be shared is a *ración*, and half of this, a *media-ración*. To substitute for a conventional main course, choose perhaps three different items. Bars specialising in tapas are places where tapas grazing *(el tapeo)* is the order of the day. Two good central areas are La Latina and Huertas, but there are good bars everywhere. Bear in mind that these days tapas are rarely free, and do not come cheap.

More than two centuries old, with bulls' heads and other taurine memorabilia on the walls, **Taberna de Antonio Sánchez** (Mesón de Paredes 13) is legendary. **Taberna Almendro 13** (Calle Almendro 13) is a great corner bar specialising in *fino* and *manzanilla* (dry sherry) and serving a wide variety of tapas and *raciones* to a noisy local crowd. **Casa del Labra** (Calle de Tetuán 12) is a great old spot near the Puerta del Sol, where the Socialist party was founded, and still serves home-made salt-cod *croquetas* and *soldados de Pavia* (salt-cod fried in batter). More sophisticated is **Bocaito** (Calle de la Libertad 6), which serves stylish Andalusian tapas from its double-sided bar.

## TO HELP YOU ORDER...

Could we have a table **¿Nos puede dar una mesa, por favor?**
Do you have a set menu? **¿Hay un menú del día?**
The menu, please **La carta, por favor**
The bill, please **La cuenta, por favor**
I'd like a/an/some… **Me gustaría pedir…**

## THE BASICS...

| | |
|---|---|
| beer **cerveza/caña** | napkin **servilleta** |
| bread **pan** | plate **plato** |
| cutlery **los cubiertos** | potatoes **patatas** |
| dessert **postre** | rice **arroz** |
| fish **pescado** | salad **ensalada** |
| fruit **fruta** | sandwich **bocadillo** |
| glass **vaso/copà** | sugar **azúcar** |
| ice cream **helado** | tea **té** |
| meat **carne** | water (chilled) **agua (fresca)** |
| mineral water **agua mineral** | wine **vino** |

## ...AND READ THE MENU

| | |
|---|---|
| **albondigas** meatballs | **langosta** spiny lobster |
| **almejas** clams | **lechón/cochinillo** suckling pig |
| **anchoas** anchovies | |
| **atún/bonito** tuna | **mariscos** shellfish |
| **calamares** squid | **ostras** oysters |
| **cangrejo** crab | **pimiento** bell pepper |
| **caracoles** snails | **pollo** chicken |
| **cerdo** pork | **pulpo** octopus |
| **chuleta** chop/cutlet | **salsa** sauce |
| **cordero** lamb | **tarta** cake |
| **entremeses** hors d'oeuvres | **ternera** veal |
| | **trucha** trout |
| **gambas** prawns | **uvas** grapes |
| **judías** beans | **verduras** vegetables |

# PLACES TO EAT

*The restaurant categories below reflect the cost of a three-course meal (starter, main course and dessert) plus a glass of house wine. Tax (IVA) is not included. 'L' means lunch, 'D' stands for dinner. At lunchtime, however, the majority of restaurants offer inexpensive two- or three-course fixed-priced menus (menú del día or menú de la casa), usually with two or three options for each course, making this, the main meal of the day, extremely affordable.*

€€€€ over 50 euros      €€€ 35–50 euros
€€ 20–35 euros      € below 20 euros

## PLAZA MAYOR AND LA LATINA

**Botín €€€** *Calle de Cuchilleros 17, tel: 91-366 4217. Open daily all year for L and D, www.botin.es.* Botín claims to be world's oldest continuously running restaurant, having opened in 1725. Many clients are visitors to the city, but Spaniards are fans too. The nooks and crannies of the old dining rooms are appealing. The roast suckling pig and roast leg of lamb prepared in wood ovens give a great taste of traditional Castilian cooking, but the menu is much more wide-ranging.

**Casa Lucío €€€** *Cava Baja 35, tel: 91-365 3252. Open Sun–Fri L and D, Sat D only. Closed Aug, www.casalucio.es.* A famous cave-like tavern with hanging cured hams, popular with affluent locals and visitors alike. High-quality Castilian cuisine: specialities include their legendary eggs with cured ham (*huevos estrellados*).

**Casa Paco €€€** *Puerta Cerrada 11, tel: 91-366 3166. Open Mon–Sat L and D, Sun L only, www.casapaco1933.com.* A classic, 75-year-old eatery serving up beef, priced by weight, seared and usually served very pink, grilled fish and, downstairs in the bar, cheese and cured ham. Attracts a stylish crowd.

**Julián de Tolosa €€€€** *Cava Baja 18, tel: 91-365 8210. Open Mon–Sat L and D, Sun L only, www.casajuliandetolosa.com.* Superb plain

Basque cooking: the huge charcoal-grilled rib steaks (*chuletón*) for two are a star dish, but the hake, black beans and red peppers are also good. Pricy but an eating experience.

## HUERTAS, SANTA ANA AND LAVAPIÉS

**Cantina Alhambra €** *Calle Victoria 9, tel: 91-521 0708. Open daily for L and D, www.tabernaalhambra.com.* Decoratively tiled bar on a side street near Plaza Santa Ana. Established in 1929, it serves great Andalusian cooking, simple but well done. Aperitivos are free with drinks and the main dishes, from paella to fried goat's cheese, are evenly good at extraordinarily fair prices.

**Casa Alberto €€** *Calle de las Huertas 18, tel: 91-429 9356. Open Tue–Sat for L and D, Sun L only, www.casaalberto.es.* An 1827 tavern where Cervantes legendarily lived, this is a good place for tapas and beer pulled from an antique tap, or a sit-down meal. Meatballs, salt cod with red peppers and beef fillet are good choices.

**Cerveceria Alemana €–€€** *Plaza Santa Ana 6, tel: 91-429 7033. Open Wed–Mon for L and D. Closed Aug, www.cerveceriaalemana. com.* Whatever the service and food are like – both could be improved – this place is an unmissable visit for some because of its connections with Hemingway. There's a good range of beers and an acceptable choice of home-made tapas and raciones (bigger portions). Food until 2am at weekends.

**La Musa de Espronceda €–€€** *Sta Isabel 17, tel: 91-539 1284. Open Tue–Sat L and D, Sun L only.* A short stroll from the Reina Sofia, this buzzy young bar-restaurant serves great set-lunches and creative Basque style tapas, called *pinchos*, until past midnight to an arts crowd. Friday and Saturday evenings see up to fifty choices laid out on the bar. Excellent service.

## PALACIO REAL AND OPERA

**La Bola €€** *Calle de la Bola 5, tel: 91-547 6930. Open Mon–Sat for L and D, Sun L only, www.labola.es.* This tiny, bright red restaurant on the corner of Calle de la Bola is a Madrid institution for its cocido, cooked in individual earthenware pots. Good shellfish and grilled meats and fish, too. Wonderful atmosphere. No credit cards.

**Café de Oriente €–€€** *Plaza de Oriente 2, tel: 91-541 3974. Open daily for L and D.* Staying open late (the café serves until 1.30am Mon–Thur and Sun, and until 2.30am Fri–Sat), this brasserie is in a great location next to the Opera House, with summer terrace. Classic international cooking. Pricy, but good for a late coffee or drink.

**Cornucopia €€** *Calle Navas de Tolosa 9, tel: 91-521 3896. Open daily for L and D, www.restaurantecornucopia.com.* This elegant and delightful restaurant serves excellent, beautifully presented modern world cooking. Lovely desserts, home-made bread and bargain lunchtime set menu.

**Taberna del Alabardero €€€** *Calle Felipe V 4–6, tel: 91-547 2577. Open daily for L and D, www.tabernadelalabardero.com.* This classic tavern, owned by a priest, is a good place to visit after a night at the opera or for a rejuvenating lunch after touring the Palacio Real. It's a bustling tapas bar at the front and, at the back, a more select Basque restaurant serving fresh fish and exquisite meat dishes till midnight.

## SOL, GRAN VIA AND CHUECA

**Artemisa €** *Ventura de la Vega 4 and Tres Cruces 4, tel: 91-429 5092 and 91-521 8721. Open daily for L and D, www.restaurantes vegetarianosartemisa.com.* A good central vegetarian option, with two branches near the Prado and Gran Vía, serves creative dishes with very fresh ingredients. The lunch menu is very popular with nearby office workers. Rustic decor. Good wines, some organic.

**Bocaito €€** *Calle de la Libertad 4–6, tel: 91-532 1219. Open Mon–Fri L and D, Sat D only. Closed Aug, www.bocaito.com.* One of the city's best traditional tapas bars, in the heart of Chueca. You can assemble a meal from the great tapas including croquettes, garlic prawns and octopus, or try the main courses in the restaurant, behind the double bar, featuring Castilian and Andalusian specialities.

**Café del Círculo de Bellas Artes** €€ *Marqués de Casa Riera 2, tel: 91-360 5400. Open all day daily (till 3am Fri and Sat).* It costs €1 to become a day member at the Círculo de Bellas Artes, which gives access to the cultural society's gorgeous cafetería/bar. Think huge chandeliers, marble statues, vast windows onto Alcalá. The set lunch is the best of the eating, but there is a great atmosphere. Summer terrace.

**Home Burger** € *Calle San Marcos 26, tel: 91-521 8531. Mon–Thur 1.30–4pm, 8.30pm–midnight, Fri and Sat 1.30pm–midnight, Sun 1.30pm–11pm, www.homeburgerbar.com.* A small chain of organic burger bars offering simple gourmet variations like different cheese toppings, good wine and real chips. Of the four branches, this one, just off the Gran Vía, has a good soundtrack and jokey décor (don't miss the basement).

**Lhardy** €€€€ *Carrera de San Jerónimo 8, tel: 91-522 2207. Open Mon–Sat for L and D, Sun L only, www.lhardy.com.* Founded in 1839, Lhardy is part of Madrid's history, with formal 19th-century dining rooms upstairs and below a deli and tapas bar where you can enjoy pastries and consommé. The cocido is famous.

**La Terraza del Casino** €€€€ *Alcalá 15, tel: 91-532 1275. Open Mon–Fri L and D, Sat D only.* Paco Roncero's avant-garde cooking in the El Bullí avant-garde school, yet personalised, draws a stylish crowd to this grand dining room. Great wines and service.

**Zara** €€ *Infantas 5, tel: 91-532 2074. Open Mon–Fri L and D. Closed Aug, www.restaurantezara.com.* For something different, try this packed restaurant serving Cuban beans, stews and daiquiris in a genuine family atmosphere. You may need to queue (it's worth it).

## SALAMANCA, CASTELLANA AND PRADO

**Astrid and Gastón,** €€€ *Po de la Castellana 13, tel 91-702 6262. Open daily 1.30–3.30pm, 8.30–11.30pm, www.astridandgaston.com.* Gaston Acurio, chef and food campaigner, launched Peruvian cuisine from this restaurant, now a classic for authentic *ceviches, pisco, tiraditos* and other dishes in an elegant urban dining room.

**Combarro €€€€** *Ortega y Gasset 40, tel: 91-577 4654. Open Mon–Sat L and D, www.combarro.com.* Superb fish and shellfish flown in daily from Spain's four seas, simply cooked to show off the quality. If you love shellfish this is worth every penny of the steep bill.

**Café Gijón €€€** *Paseo de Recoletos 21, tel: 91-521 5425. Open 7am–1am daily, www.cafegijon.com.* Legendary literary café fashionable with arty types since it opened in 1888. It still serves as a meeting place at any time of day, for a coffee or drink, lunch or supper. Two set-price menus or carte. One pays for the cachet.

**Diverxo €€€€** *Calle Pensamiento 28, tel: 91-570 0766. Open Tue–Sat 1.30–4pm, 9–11.30pm, www.diverxo.com.* Currently rated as Madrid's top avant-garde kitchen, producing four tasting menus adapted to each table's tastes. The dozen or so dishes in each are beautiful to the eye and explore intriguing global flavours. Booking by email (info@diverxo.com) advised one month ahead.

**Santceloni €€€€** *Po de la Castellana, 57, tel: 91-210 8840. Open Mon–Fri 2–4pm, 8–11pm, Sat D, www.restaurantesantceloni.com.* Madrid's most stylish hotel restaurant, masterminded by the late Catalan star-chef Santi Santamaría, with tasting menus that strike a fine balance between tradition and creativity, plus a cheese trolley to die for. Good wines and service.

**Sergi Arola Gastro €€€€** *Zurbano 31, tel: 91-310 2169. Open Mon–Fri and hols L and D, Sat D only, closed Christmas and New Year, www.sergiarola.com.* Designer gourmet bistro offering a series of set menus, from avant-garde to food for cheese lovers, with a scale of prices that acknowledge the market for Michelin star eating with value.

## OUTSIDE MADRID

## ÁVILA

**El Molino de la Losa €€€** *Bajada de la Losa 12, tel: 920-211 101. Open daily for L and D, closed Sun D, closed Nov–Apr, www.elmolino*

*delalosa.com*. Enjoy great views from this ancient mill on an island in the river. Classic and modern cuisine.

## SAN LORENZO EL ESCORIAL

**El Charolés €€€** *Calle Floridablanca 24, tel: 91-890 5975. Open daily for L and D, closed Christmas Eve and New Year's Eve.* Inventive market cooking and a comprehensive wine list. Serves cocido on Wednesday and Friday, except for fiesta days. Luscious lemon and honey ice cream.

## SEGOVIA

**Mesón de Cándido €€–€€€** *Plaza Azoguejo 5, tel: 921-425 911. Open daily for L and D, www.mesondecandido.com.* This family-run restaurant in the shadow of the aqueduct has been an inn since the 18th century and was made a national monument in 1941. Legendary wood-roast meats.

**Restaurante José María €€€** *Cronista Lecea 11, tel: 921-461 111. Open daily for L and D, www.rtejosemaria.com.* A good place whether you're just peckish or starving, as there's a busy tapas bar at the front and a relaxed restaurant. Try Segovian roasts or excellent fish dishes based on Atlantic produce. Tasting menu.

**Hostal del Cardenal €€€** *Paseo Recaredo 24, tel: 925-224 900. Open daily for L and D, www.hostaldelcardenal.com.* The restaurant associated with the lovely hotel of the same name has long been one of Toledo's top kitchens. Best known for its wood roasts. Delightful summer terrace.

## TOLEDO

**Restaurante Adolfo €–€€** *Calle Hombre de Palo 7, tel: 925-227 321. Open Tue–Sat for L and D, Sun L only, www.adolforestaurante. com.* Toledo haute cuisine is served in a medieval building near the cathedral. Game is a speciality; the huge wine cellar is the city's finest.

# A–Z TRAVEL TIPS

## A Summary of Practical Information

# A

## ACCOMMODATION

Spanish hotels are rated by a star system, with five-star deluxe the top grade. The classifications often seem arbitrary; some two- and three-star places will be of the same quality as a hotel with a higher rating. About two-thirds of the city's hotels fall into the three- and four-star categories. Breakfast (usually a continental-style buffet) is rarely included in the room rate.

I'd like a double/single room. **Me gustaría pedir una habitación doble/sencilla**
with/without bath/shower **con/sin baño/ducha**
double bed **cama matrimonial**
What's the rate per night? **¿Cuál es el precio por noche?**
Is breakfast included? **¿Está incluído el desayuno?**

Hotel reservation desks are found at Barajas Airport, at Chamartín and Atocha railway stations, and in the Torre de Madrid on Plaza de España. Before taking a room, the guest fills out a form, which states the hotel category, room number and price, and signs it. Winter months (Nov–Mar) are formally the low season, but in practise prices often vary through the year, between weekends and weekdays, and according to booking levels. Outside the city top-flight accommodation is not as easy to find and is best booked in advance.

## AIRPORT

**Barajas International Airport** (MAD, www.aena.es), 16km (10 miles) east of Madrid, handles domestic and international flights. Currently Terminals 1 and 4 are for international flights (Terminal 1 handles most charter flights, Easyjet and Air France; Terminal 4 handles Iberia, British Airways, Lan, Avianco and Vueling); Terminal

2 for domestic flights and Iberia's Central European services; and Terminal 3 for the Barcelona Shuttle and Spanish regional carriers.

Coming through Arrivals *(Llegadas)* is quick; leaving through Departures *(Salidas)* is slow – allow plenty of time.

Taxis are available outside all terminals and cost from €18 to €35 depending on which part of the city you are going to, the amount of luggage, day and time of travel (an extra 20 percent is charged on Sunday). Generally allow 20–30 minutes to reach the city centre. The cheaper, equally reliable option is the 24-hour Autobús Express Aeropuerto, travelling either way in 15–20 minutes, with central drop-off and pick-up points at Plaza de Cibeles and Atocha railway station (charge €5).

Another inexpensive option, useful when traffic is heavy, is the Metro from the airport to Nuevos Ministerios station north of the city centre (journey time about 14 minutes). From here a change to Line 10 takes you to Plaza de España in about 15 minutes. A single ticket costs €4. Alternatively, buy a 10-in-one ticket, or *Abono*, for around €12, plus the airport supplement. Trains run from 6am–midnight.

## B

### BICYCLE RENTAL

Although Madrid has few cycle lanes, travelling by bicycle through the parks, pedestrianised streets and old quarter's quiet lanes is safe and pleasant, especially in good weather. Among various companies that offer bicycles for hire, Trixi (www.trixi.com) is very central and also offers tours and skateboards.

### BUDGETING FOR YOUR TRIP

There are numerous ways to save money by planning ahead. Flight prices may be a quarter of the price midweek. Local transport services and the municipal, royal and regional tourist bodies make changing offers that are worth researching ahead of time. These include flat-price tickets for limitless metro and rail travel, cut-price long-distance rail travel rates for advance booking. The MadridCard (www.madridcard) is the essential pass for visitors and includes entry to over 50 museums and monuments with discounts in shops and restaurants. Available online at different prices for 24, 48, 72 or 120 hours, with reduced rates for children.

By sticking to the excellent set-menus offered by bars and restaurants you can keep your food expenses to a fixed budget.

## C

### CAMPING

Madrid has an excellent year-round camping site a short metro or bus ride east of the city, at Alameda de Osuna. Camping Osuna, Jardines de Aranjuez 1, tel: 91-741 050, metro Canillejas / El Capricho (www.campingosuna.com), rents spaces for tents and caravans. Facilities include a good bar-restaurant and small supermarket.

### CAR HIRE

To hire a car in Spain, you must usually be at least 23 years of age, with either an international driving licence or a valid licence from your own country. All motorcycle riders must wear helmets and ride with their headlights on, even during the day. Car hire must be paid for with a major credit card unless you leave a large deposit. Third-party insurance will be included; fully comprehensive may cost extra.

I'd like to hire a car (tomorrow). **Me gustaría pedir alquiler un coche (para mañana).**
for one day/a week **por un día/una semana**
Please include full insurance. **Haga el favor de incluir el seguro a todo riesgo.**
Unleaded petrol **gasolina sin plomo**
Fill it up **Lleno, por favor**

Cars can be hired per day with an additional fee according to mileage, or in package deals for a set number of days at unlimited mileage. The average daily cost for a middle-range car (Peugeot 306) with unlimited mileage and full insurance is around €40–60.

Car hire agencies include:

**Atesa** Pl de España (carpark), tel: 915-542 5015; www.atesa.es

**Avis** Gran Vía 60, tel: 91-547 2048; www.avis.com

**Europcar** Po de la Castellana 193, tel: 902-503 010; www.europcar.com

**Hertz** Pl de España 18, tel: 91-542 5805; www.hertz.es

**Sixt** Rda de Atocha 5, tel: 902-491 616; www.sixt.es

## CLIMATE

You'd be wise to avoid Madrid in July and August, as many Madrileños do, unless you like stifling heat. Many restaurants and sites of interest close completely. In the winter months, Madrid can be very cold at times, too, with sub-zero temperatures, snow, and icy winds.

Spring, early summer or autumn are the best seasons to travel to Madrid – you're likely to experience ideal temperatures, low humidity and some of the brightest sunshine in Europe.

## CLOTHING

Madrid's traditional smartness of dress has relaxed. Businessmen often wear an open-collar shirt in summer. But, resort wear would be inappropriate in this big city and attracts stares when worn by the unwary. A few upper-echelon restaurants require jackets and ties for men. On visits to churches, it's best to wear modest cover-up clothing though in the heat of summer, no one is likely to prohibit men from entering in walking shorts.

## CRIME AND SAFETY

Though Madrid is no more dangerous than any other capital city, tourists should be on guard, especially close to the Prado (where scams are often perpetrated), the Rastro, Gran Vía, Puerta del Sol,

Plaza Mayor, Plaza de Toros bullring, on the Metro or at any large street gathering. The most common crimes are pickpocketing and the snatching of passports and handbags.

As ever, it pays to be careful. Do not leave luggage unattended; don't carry more money on your person than you'll need for daily expenses; use the hotel safe deposit for larger sums and valuables; in crowds around street attractions and sports events, be on your guard against pickpockets; reject offers of flowers or other objects from street pedlars–they may be after your purse; don't leave valuables in view inside your car, even when it's locked; photocopy personal documents and leave the originals in your hotel.

> I want to report a theft. Quiero denunciar un robo.
> My ticket/wallet/passport/purse has been stolen. Me han
>     robado mi billete/cartera/pasaporte/monadera

If you are robbed, contact the local police station or dial 092 for the city police *(policía municipal)*.

## DRIVING

Crossing the border into Spain, you won't be asked for documents, but in the event of any problem you will have to produce your passport, driving licence, registration papers and insurance documents, which must be carried with you at all times when driving.

> **¡Alto!** Stop!
> **Aparcamiento** Parking
> **Autopista** Motorway
> **Ceda el paso** Give way (yield)

**Cruce peligroso** Dangerous crossroads
**Curva peligrosa** Dangerous bend
**Despacio** Slow
**Peligro** Danger
**Prohibido adelantar** No overtaking (passing)
**Prohibido aparcar** No parking
**Sentido único** One way (street)

Avoid driving in Madrid. Nerve-wracking traffic jams are a way of life, although there is a lull between 3.00 and 4.30pm. There are many accidents on the streets in the early hours of the morning, when the clubs close. Madrid drivers are not noted for their courtesy.

**Rules and Regulations**. You should display a nationality sticker on your car. Most fines for traffic offences are payable on the spot or at a bank within a set time limit. Driving rules are the same as throughout Spain: drive on the right, overtake (pass) on the left, yield right of way to vehicles coming from the right (unless your road is marked as having priority). Front and rear seat belts are compulsory.

Speed limits are 120km/h (75mph) on motorways, 100km/h (62mph) on broad main roads (two lanes each way), 90km/h (56mph) on other main roads, 50km/h (31mph), or as marked, in densely populated areas.

**If You Need Help**. Garages are efficient, but repairs may take time in busy areas. Spare parts are readily available for Spanish-built cars and many other popular models. For less-common makes, they may have to be imported. For emergencies, tel: 091.

# E

## ELECTRICITY

The standard electric current is 220 volts, but some hotels have a voltage of 110–120 in bathrooms as a safety precaution. Check before plugging in any appliance. Sockets (outlets) take round, two-pin plugs, so you will probably need an international adapter plug.

## EMBASSIES AND CONSULATES

Many Western European countries have embassies in Madrid. Some useful addresses are as follows:

**Australia**: Plaza del Descubridor 3, tel: 91-353 6600, www.spain. embassy.gov.au

**Canada**: Calle Núñez de Balboa 35, tel: 91-423 3250, www.canada international.gc.ca

**Ireland**: Paseo de la Castellana 46, tel: 91-436 4093, www.embassyof ireland.es

**New Zealand**: Plaza de la Lealtad 2, tel: 91-523 0226, www.nz embassy.com

**UK**: Calle Fernando el Santo 16, tel: 91-700 8200, www.ukinspaiin. fco.gov.uk (NB: Citizens of Commonwealth countries may apply to the UK embassy.)

**United States**: Calle de Serrano 75, tel: 91-587 2200, www.spanish. madrid.usembassy.gov

## EMERGENCIES (see also Health and Medical Care and Police)

In the event of an emergency, contact the relevant source of assistance:

**Coordinated Emergency Number** 112
**Emergency Medical Care** 112
**Ambulance** 061 or 901 222 222 (Red Cross/Croz Roja)
**City Police** 092
**Fire Service (Madrid)** 080

**G**

## GAY AND LESBIAN TRAVELLERS

Madrid has a vibrant gay and lesbian scene, which is centred in the neighbourhood of Chueca, whose grid of narrow lanes lies just north of the Gran Vía. The local multitude of bars and clubs vary from low-key to hardcore, and magazines on gay social life, such as *Shangay Expres* and *Odisea*, give further information. This *barrio's* small café-lined central square is a hive of hetero-gay activity during the summer and is a good place to meet people.

Gay Pride week, at the end of June, includes a high-heels race and a Saturday procession with floats that is a hugely popular fiesta with young and old alike, bringing the city centre to a standstill.

## GETTING THERE (see also Airport and Driving)

**By Air**. Madrid's airport Barajas is linked by daily non-stop flights from across Europe. Most flights from the US and Canada are direct; others stop first in Lisbon, Frankfurt or London. From Australia and New Zealand, regular one-stop flights go directly to Madrid.

There are direct flights to Madrid from the UK via British Airways (www.ba.com) and Iberia (www.iberia.es), as well as low-cost Easyjet (www.easyjet.com) and Ryanair (www.ryanair.com) flights from airports outside London. There are services between Madrid and the United States with Iberia, TWA, Continental, United, Delta and American Airlines (www.americanairlines.com).

Domestic services are operated by Iberia (tel: 902-400 500), Vueling (tel: 902-333 933) and Ryanair (www.ryanair.com).

**By Road**. The main access road from France to Madrid skirts the western end of the Pyrenees. A motorway (expressway) runs from Biarritz (France) through the Basque Country via Bilbao to Burgos, from where you take the E25 motorway straight down to Madrid, 240km (150 miles) away.

Express coach services operate between London and Madrid as well as between other European cities and Madrid. For further details, visit www.eurlines.co.uk.

**By Rail**. Anyone travelling from the UK should take the Eurostar to Paris, from where there are overnight trains to Madrid. For discounts and special rail tickets, see page 132.

## GUIDES AND TOURS

The Centro de Turismo de Madrid (City Tourism Office, Plaza Mayor 27, tel: 91-454 4410; daily 9.30am–8.30pm) offers personal advice, a database and historical and cultural tours by bus and on foot throughout the year, covering a wide array of topics and sights. Unless there's a large English-speaking group, though, tours are conducted in Spanish. Madrid City Tour (tel: 902-024 758; www.madrid-citytour.es) organises hop-on, hop-off multi-language city bus tours that depart from the Prado daily Nov–Feb 10am–6pm, Mar–Oct 9am–10pm.

There are three main companies organising coach tours to Aranjuez, El Escorial, Toledo, Ávila and Segovia:

**Pullmantur** Plaza de Oriente 8 (Metro: Opera), tel: 91-541 1807, www.pullmantur.es

**Trapsatur** San Bernardo 5–7 (Metro: Santo Domingo), tel: 91-541 6321, www.trapsatur.es

**Juliatur** Gran Vía, 68 (Metro: Plaza de España), tel: 91-559 9605, www.juliatours.es

# H

## HEALTH AND MEDICAL CARE

Standards of hygiene are high, and medical care in Madrid is excellent. Most doctors speak sufficient English to deal with foreign patients. The water is safe to drink, but bottled water is always safest, and is available everywhere. Most local people drink bottled water, *agua con gas* (carbonated) or *sin gas* (still). It is good, clean and inexpensive.

Visitors from EU countries with corresponding health-insurance facilities are entitled to medical and hospital treatment under the Spanish social security system. You must have your European Health Insurance Card (EHIC) card with you for reciprocal health care. Before travelling, British subjects should obtain an EHIC card (forms available at post offices, online at www.ehic.org.uk, or tel: 0845 606 2030).

It is recommended that you also take out reputable private medical insurance, which will be part of almost all travel insurance packages.

Chemists (*farmacias*) operate as a first line of defence for Spaniards, as pharmacists can prescribe drugs and are usually adept at making on-the-spot diagnoses. Pharmacies, marked by a green neon cross lit up when open, operate during normal business hours and one in every district remains open all night and on holidays. The location and phone number of this *farmacia de guardia* is posted on the door of all the other pharmacies. All-night pharmacies can also be contacted by calling 098. To locate a hospital or report a medical emergency, dial 112.

If you take drugs on prescription, ensure that you take extra supplies with you. Spanish chemists do not honour foreign prescriptions. Given the dry climate and sun levels, it is a good idea to wear sunscreen and carry water with you in both summer and winter.

## L

### LANGUAGE

After Chinese and English, the most widely spoken language in the world is Spanish, from Madrid to Manila, from Ávila to Argentina. The Castilian spoken in Madrid is understood in most areas of Spain, although Catalan, Basque, Gallego and Valencian are official languages in their home areas. It's certainly worth learning a few basic phrases and the *Berlitz Spanish Phrasebook and Dictionary* covers all situations you are likely to encounter in your travels in Spain.

##  M

### MAPS

A free street map covering the whole of Madrid is available at Tourist Information Offices at the airport, railway stations and in the city. It is sufficient for virtually all city travel. Visitors should also pick up the pocket-sized map of the Metro underground system (*un plano del metro*), available free at any Metro station.

## MEDIA

**Television**. There are four nationwide television channels in Spain, TVE-1, La 2 (public), Cuatro, La Sexta, Antena 3 and Tele 5. Many hotels offer Canal Plus and its linked channels. In Madrid, you can also watch Telemadrid, which often offers the dual option of watching films in their original language.

Most programmes are in Spanish with the occasional late-night film in the original language. Many hotels have access to a wider range of satellite stations.

**Print media**. The Spanish quality national daily papers (*periódicos*) sold in Madrid include *El País, La Vanguardia, ABC* and *El Mundo*. They provide full local information on cinema, theatre, regular and satellite television programming, and list chemist shops that are open late at night. *El Mundo* includes handy supplements with its Friday edition, giving listings on exhibitions, art shows and film schedules, along with lists of restaurants, entertainment and television. El País publishes a similar supplement on Friday, called *Tentaciones*. These are along the lines of the weekly, all-encompassing *Guía del Ocio (Guide to Leisure)*.

You will also be able to find the *International Herald Tribune* and *Time* and *Newsweek* magazines at major newsstands. Other papers, such as *The Times, Guardian* and *Wall Street Journal*, can be purchased at larger stands, particularly around the Puerta del Sol.

## MONEY

The currency of Spain is the euro, which comes in coins valued 1 euro, 2 euros, plus 50, 20, 10, 5, 2 and 1 cents. Bills are in denominations of 5, 10, 20, 50, 100, 200 and 500 euros.

**Credit Cards**. These are used extensively in Spain and most towns have cashpoint facilities, which are generally the cheapest way to change cash, especially if you withdraw quantities of €200.

Where's the nearest bank/currency exchange office?
   **¿Dónde está el banco/la casa de cambio
   más cercana?**
I want to change some pounds/dollars. **Quiero cambiar
   libras/dólares.**
Do you accept travellers cheques? **¿Aceptan cheques de
   viajero?**
Can I pay with a credit card? **¿Se puede pagar con tarjeta?**
How much is that? **¿Cuánto es?**

O

## OPENING TIMES

The practice of the siesta, the long midday break and nap, is losing
adherents in Madrid, except in the hot months. The big department
stores and supermarkets remain open all day. Still, very few small
shops remain open all day; their usual hours are from 9.30am–1.30
or 2pm and 4.30 or 5–8pm, Mon–Sat. Some shops close on Saturday
afternoons. Increasingly department stores and high street chain outlets open on Sundays. Major museums are now shifting to unbroken
day-long opening.

Restaurants serve lunch from 1–4pm; in the evening their timing
depends on the kind of customers they expect. Local people usually
eat between 9 and 11pm or later. Places catering to foreigners may
function from 7pm on, and many stay open throughout the day.

Banks are usually Mon–Fri 8.30 or 9.00am–2pm. Savings banks
such as La Caixa open on Tuesday evening. Some banks open Saturday 9am–1pm apart from those that open Thursday evening. All
banks close on Saturday afternoon, Sunday and fiestas. Government
offices and most businesses are open from 9am–2pm and from 3pm
to anywhere from 5.30–7pm; summer hours mid-June to mid-Sept
are 8am–3pm.

# P

## POLICE

Spanish municipal and national police are efficient, strict and courteous – and generally very responsive to issues involving foreign tourists. In Madrid, dial 092 for municipal police and 091 for national police. The central police station (Policía Nacional), with interpreters, is located at Calle Leganitos 19, near Plaza de España (tel: 902-102 112).

## POST OFFICES

Post offices (correos) are identified by yellow-and-white signs with a crown and the words 'Correos y Telégrafos'. District post offices open Mon–Fri 9am–2pm and Sat 9am–1pm. The central post office on Calle de Montalban 1, is open Mon–Fri 8.30am–9.30pm (tel: 91-523 0694). Most post offices close at 8.30pm, but El Corte Ingles has instore post offices open throughout their retailing hours including Sundays.

In postal addresses, note that s/n ('sin numero') means that the full address does not include a street number.

## PUBLIC HOLIDAYS

1 January **Año Nuevo** New Year's Day
6 January **Epifanía** Epiphany
20 January **San Sebastián** St Sebastian's Day
1 May **Fiesta del Trabajo** Labour Day
25 July **Santiago Apóstol** St James's Day
15 August **Asunción** Assumption
12 October **Día de la Hispanidad** Discovery of America Day (Spanish National Day)
1 November **Todos los Santos** All Saints' Day
6 December **Día de la Constitución** Constitution Day
8 December **Inmaculada Concepción** Immaculate Conception

25 December **Navidad** Christmas Day
26 December **La Fiesta Navidad** Christmas Holiday
**Movable dates:**
**Jueves Santo** Holy Thursday
**Viernes Santo** Good Friday
**Lunes de Pascua** Easter Monday
**Corpus Christi** Corpus Christi
In addition to these nationwide holidays, there are big celebrations
in Madrid on 2 May (El Dos de Mayo), and public holidays on 15
May, the city's patron saint's day (San Isidro Labrador/St Isidore the
Husbandman), and on 9 November, La Almudena.

## R

### RELIGION

The national religion of Spain is Roman Catholicism, and Mass is
said regularly in the churches of Madrid. There are churches of most
major faiths; the tourist information offices have information on religious services, including those in foreign languages. Note that many
churches open only for mass.

## T

### TELEPHONES

Spain's country code is 34. Madrid's local area code, 91, must be di-
alled before all phone numbers, even for local calls. To make a direct
overseas call, first dial 00 and then dial the country and city codes.

There are various options for making a call from Madrid. You
can make direct-dial local and international calls from Telefónica's
public phone booths *(cabinas)* in the street. Most operate with both
coins and cards *(tarjetas telefónicas, available from tobacconists. International telephone credit cards can also be used. To make a call,
pick up the receiver, wait for the tone, deposit your money or in-

sert your card and dial the number. Most bars have coin-operated or meter telephones available for public use as well. Post office telephones and internet bureaux known as *locutorios* are often the cheapest option of all.

The main international mobile operators in Spain are Vodafone, Orange and Yoigo. The main Spanish operator is Movistar. Roaming fees, depending on your contract, will appear as a message when you switch on your phone in Spain. At mobile operators' city centre outlets you can buy SIM cards, seek technical help or buy pay-as-you-go phones which may be topped up at many shops and cybercafés.

## TIME ZONES

Spanish time coincides with the rest of Western Europe – Greenwich Mean Time plus one hour. In spring, another hour is added for Daylight Saving Time (Summer Time).

## TIPPING

Service is usually included in restaurant bills, but it is customary to leave the spare change in the dish when eating at a modest restaurant and a few cents at a bar. When dining at a fairly smart restaurant, an additional 5–10 percent of the bill is appropriate. Small change or a 10 percent tip is fine for an average taxi ride.

## TOILETS

Toilet doors are distinguished by a 'C' for *Caballeros* (gentlemen) or 'S' for *Señoras* (ladies) or by a variety of pictographs (often amusing).

Where are the toilets? **¿Dónde están los servicios?**

## TOURIST INFORMATION

**UK**: 22–3 Manchester Square, London W1M 5AP; tel: 020-7486 8077; www.tourspain.co.uk.

**US**: 1395 Brickell Avenue, Suite 1130, Miami, FL 33131, tel: 305-358 1992; Water Tower Place, Suite 915 East, 845 North Michigan Ave, Chicago, IL 60611, tel: 312-642 1992; 8383 Wilshire Blvd, Suite 960, 90211 Beverly Hills, CA 90211; tel: 323-658 7188; 666 Fifth Ave, 35th floor, New York, NY 10103; tel: 212-265 8822; www.okspain.org.

**Canada**: 2 Bloor St. West, Suite 3402, Toronto, Ontario M4W 3E2; tel: 1416-961 3131; www.spain.info/en_CA.

**In Spain**:

Tourist information for all of Spain is available at the Madrid tourist offices (*oficinas de información turística*) in Barajas airport (T1 and 4 arrivals); at Duque de Medinaceli 2; in Chamartín station, Door 10; and in Atocha station, close to the AVE platforms. All open Mon–Fri 9am–7 or 8 pm, Sat 9am–1pm.

The main Madrid city tourist office is at Plaza Mayor 27 (Casa de Panadería), tel: 91-588 1635, and is open daily 10am–8pm, Sat 10am–3pm. There are information kiosks in Plaza de Cibeles; Plaza de Callao; Centro Arte Reina Sofía and Plaza de Colón (underpass). All open at 10am and close between 7.30 and 8.30pm

For telephone information on tourist facilities and practical matters, tel: 010 for the City Information Office, 012 for information on Madrid region.

## TRANSPORT

Madrid has a reliable and comprehensive public transport system. Getting around town, especially by Metro (subway/tube) is easy, rapid, and inexpensive. Collect up-to-date Metro and train maps from station ticket offices. One website provides information for all services: www.ctm-madrid.es.

**Buses** (*autobuses*). Inner-city buses currently operate a set fare regardless of the route or length of journey in the city centre. You enter from the front and pay the driver or stamp your multi-journey ticket. You don't need to have the exact fare, but you should offer coins. Press the buzzer at the stop you require and leave by the rear door.

An *Abono* is good for 10 journeys by bus or Metro and works out much cheaper than buying 10 individual tickets. It can be purchased from the bus informaion booths at Puerta del Sol, Plaza Callao, Plaza de la Cibeles and Plaza de Castilla, as well as in every Metro station.

If you are planning to spend an extended period of time in Madrid and doing a lot of bus and Metro travelling, purchase an Abono. This card can be applied for at any *estanco* by filling out a form and providing a passport-size photograph and a photocopy of your passport or national identity document. It is valid for a month, with reductions for people under 18 and over 65.

Buses are in service 6am–11.30pm. For municipal bus information, tel: 91-406 8800.

**Metro**. The Madrid Metro system is the fastest, cheapest and most efficient way of getting around the city. It operates from 6am–1.30am. Most trains have air-conditioning. Central journeys currently have flat-rate tickets and you can buy a cut-rate Abono, which allows you to make 10 trips (by Metro or bus) or a 1-, 3-, 5- or 7-day *Abono Turistico*. For information, tel: 902-444 403.

**Taxis**. Madrid taxis are relatively inexpensive and plentiful. They are white, have a transversal red stripe on the sides and the Madrid coat of arms. They can be hailed with relative ease on main thoroughfares or may be found at *paradas* de taxi (taxi stands), indicated by a large white 'T' against a dark blue background, or requested by phone. They are available if they are displaying a green *libre* (free) sign on the windscreen or have a little green light on. If a red sign with the name of a Madrid neighbourhood is displayed, it means it is on its way home and not obliged to pick you up unless you are going in the same direction.

A meter on the dashboard indicates an initial fare at the start of the journey, and chalks up an extra sum for every kilometre. If you ask the driver to wait, he can charge you a set price per hour. Supplements can be added on Sunday and holidays; from 11pm–6am; for pick-up or delivery at a railway station, football stadium or bullring;

for pick-up or delivery at the race track, Club de Campo, or the Club Puerta de Hierro; for each piece of luggage and for trips to or from the airport. If you leave the municipal limits for the suburbs, the driver is entitled to ask for double the fare per kilometer as of that point.

**Trains** *(trenes)*. Spanish trains have two classes: First *(Primera* or *1ª)* and Second *(Segunda* or *2ª)*, and a variety of categories, which vary in terms of comfort. The Talgo is a fast, comfortable train with video entertainment; the TERs and Electrotrens have similar facilities, but are not as fast. On night trains, one can usually get a cama (small, private compartment) or an inexpensive *litera* (a couchette in a compartment shared with five other passengers). *Rapidos* are local day trains good for short journeys. AVEs are high-speed bullet trains that now form a good network around the country.

Madrid's northern railway station, **Chamartín**, at Avenida Pio XII in the north of the city, handles 80 percent of the city's rail traffic, including AVE services to Segovia and Valladolid. The station has a shopping and entertainment complex. The former Estación del Norte, now called **Príncipe Pío**, only operates trains to Alcalá de Henares. **Atocha** station in the south of the city operates AVE and other services to and from Andalucía, Castilla La Mancha, Extremadura and Levante (AVE journey times Seville or Malaga 2.5 hours, Toledo 30 minutes, Barcelona via Zaragoza 2.5 hours, Valencia 1 hour 40 minutes). There are shops, restaurants and a left-luggage office (daily 5.30am–10pm, opens Sat 6.15am, Sun 6.30am).

When leaving Madrid by train, check your tickets carefully, as the Estrella express night trains leave from Chamartín rather than Atocha, and services to Levante (the East Coast, including Valencia and Alicante) leave from both Atocha and Chamartín.

**Rail tickets**. There are many ways to save money on rail travel in Spain. For more information see the website of the national rail company RENFE: tel: 902-320 320; www.renfe.com.

Visitors other than Europeans and North Africans can buy a

Eurail pass (www.eurail.com). It allows unlimited first or second-class travel throughout Spain and 22 other participating countries. These must be purchased before your arrival in Europe.

Europeans and North Africans can take advantage of the Interrail scheme (www.interrail.com) which permits unlimited second-class travel in up to 30 European and North African countries.

If you don't have a Eurail or Interrail pass, you can buy a RENFE Spain pass offering 4–12 journeys during a calendar month at fixed prices.

It is worth asking the RENFE office about discounts for advance booking, especially by web, which rise to 60 percent for certain routes and trains. Ask at stations or see www.renfe.com for details.

When's the next train to…? **¿Cuándo sale el próximo tren para…?**
A ticket to… **Un billete para…**
single (one-way) **ida**
return (round-trip) **ida y vuelta**
What's the fare to…? **¿Cuánto es la tarifa a …?**

## VISAS AND ENTRY REQUIREMENTS

Visitors from the EU (and citizens of Andorra, Liechtenstein, Monaco and Switzerland) require only a valid national identity card from their home state to enter Spain. As British citizens have no identity cards, they need a passport. Citizens of the United States, Australia and New Zealand require a valid passport and are automatically authorised for a three-month stay. Visitors from elsewhere must obtain a visa from the Spanish consulate in their own country before setting off. Passport or identity card numbers are often required with flight bookings as a security measure.

Visitors can prolong a three-month stay for an additional three-month period by applying for an extension in Madrid at the Comisaría de Policía, Sección de Extranjería, Calle Los Madrazos 9.

In order to reside in Spain for an extended period a Residencia *(Visado de Residencia Serie V)* must be obtained from the Spanish embassy or consulate in one's country of origin. EU nationals are allowed to live and work in Spain, but should check residence requirements with their nearest Spanish embassy before departure.

## W

## WEBSITES AND INTERNET ACCESS

There is free internet access in the Plaza Mayor tourist office and numerous paying telephone and internet points (ask for a *locutorio*). Helpful websites are:

**www.tourspain.es** Site of Turespaña, the National Tourism Office.

**www.esmadrid.com** Madrid City Council's website, with links to transport and accommodation information.

**www.patrimonionacional.es** Website for numerous monuments, museums, parks and other sights owned by the Spanish royal family.

## Y

## YOUTH HOSTELS

Madrid has three youth hostels. Bookings are made through the same website (www-central-reservas@madrid.org). They are Albergue Juvenil Marcenado (Santa Cruz de Marcenado 28; tel: 91-547 4532; 72 beds); Albergue Juvenil Richard Scherrmann (Casa de Campo; tel: 91-463 5699; 130 beds) and Albergue Mejía Leguerica 91 (tel: 91-593 9688; 132 beds).

To make a booking you need an international albergues ID card. Rates are from €20–25 per person, for bed and breakfast, depending on your age.

# Recommended Hotels

Visitors to Madrid have plenty of choice with regard to where to stay in the city centre. Traditional *pensiones* (guesthouses) and *hostales* (modest, often family-owned hotels) are scattered around town. Palatial and boutique hotels are clustered in the main tourist areas: Puerta del Sol, Gran Vía, Paseo del Prado and Chueca. The following selection includes our top choices to cover a range of tastes. If you are staying in a very central hotel, particularly around the Gran Vía or Puerta del Sol, note that rooms facing onto the street can be very noisy at weekends. Interior rooms *(interiores)* may be darker, but also quieter. If you plan on staying out late you may like to check whether there is someone on the hotel reception 24 hours a day (usual, but not always the case). Wi-fi is usually available, but check first.

Most hotel rates do not include breakfast. Weekend rates and special deals are available at many hotels. Out-of-town rates can drop by up to 50 percent midweek. The rates quoted here are intended to give an indication of the cost of a double room in high season for one night.

| | |
|---|---|
| €€€€ | over 300 euros |
| €€€ | 200–300 euros |
| €€ | 100–200 euros |
| € | below 100 euros |

## SOL, PLAZA MAYOR, SANTA ANA

**Cat's Hostel €** *Calle Cañizares 6, tel: 91-369 2807, www.catshostel. com*. Cool young hostel with 200 beds in dormitories or double rooms grouped around a central Moorish patio, a basement bar and excellent location for alternative arts and nightlife.

**Hostal Madrid €** *Calle Esparteros 6, tel: 91-522 0060, www.hostal-madrid.info*. An extremely well-priced, quiet, central hostal, offering attractive, air-conditioned rooms and apartments, all with own bathrooms. Apartment 43 is particularly nice. Popular with a young crowd. 15 rooms and 4 apartments.

**Hotel Me Reina Victoria €€€** *Plaza Santa Ana 14, tel: 91-701 60 00, www.solmelia.com.* When the much-loved Reina Victoria was re-vamped, its cocktail bar and rooftop terrace and restaurant quickly became part of the smart Madrid scene. Hotel rooms are well fitted and the location is perfect for theatre, art galleries and nightlife. The decor and feel are glamorous.

**Persal €–€€** *Plaza del Angel 12, tel: 91-369 4643, www.hostalpersal. com.* One of the best *hostales* in Madrid, Persal is set in a 19th-century townhouse near the Plaza Mayor. Comfortable rooms. Friendly service. Buffet breakfast included.

**Petit Palace Posada del Peine €€** *Calle Postas 17, tel: 91-523 8151, www.hthoteles.com.* Boutique hotel in the pedestrianised old town, just off the Plaza Mayor, combining a historic atmosphere with designer and hi-tech details. 71 rooms, all with their own computer.

## PALACIO REAL AND OPERA

**Casa de Madrid €€€** *Calle Arrieta 2, tel: 91-559 5791, www.casade madrid.com.* An exquisite, romantic little hotel in the city. Beautiful antiques decorate the seven rooms. The prices are high but include many extras.

**Hotel Room Mate Mario €–€€** *Calle Campomanes 4, tel: 91-548 8548, www.room-matehotels.com.* A great hotel on a quiet side street about one minute's walk from the Opera House. The 54 rooms are stylishly designed, with modern decor, all mod cons (including air conditioning) and good-sized bathrooms. Friendly staff. Lovely big buffet breakfast. One of four Room Mate Hotels in Madrid. Highly recommended.

## GRAN VÍA, CHUECA, PLAZA DE ESPAÑA

**Best Western Arosa €€** *Calle Salud 21 (Edificio Gran Vía 29), tel: 91-532 1600, www.hotelarosa.com.* A well-run, four-star hotel just steps from Gran Vía, but insulated to keep the noise out. With handsome rooms and a comfortable lobby, the hotel feels more intimate than its size might indicate. 140 rooms.

**Hostal Miguel Angel €** *Calle San Mateo 21-2º, tel 91-447 5400.* Sparkling clean family-run hostal with newly decorated rooms overlooking a light-filled patio. There is a small salon and outer rooms are all double glazed.

**Hotel de las Letras €€–€€€** *Gran Vía 11, tel: 91-523 7980, www.hoteldelasletras.com.* Spacious designer hotel, with a stylish mix of old and new decor. Facilities such as the library, urban spa, the rooftop terrace bar, popular with locals, and Japanese cuisine, offer comfort with a difference.

**Hotel Petit Palace Ducal €€** *Calle de Hortaleza 3, tel: 91-521 1043, www.hthoteles.com.* A stylish small hotel at the southern end of Chueca's lively Calle de Hortaleza. Comfortable spacious rooms, with chic minimalist decor. 58 rooms.

**Hotel Room Mate Óscar €€€** *Plaza Vázquez de Malla 12, tel: 91-701 1173, www.room-matehotels.com.* The rooftop swimming pool, pop decor and varied designer rooms at reasonable prices have put this on the map as Chueca's hippest hotel.

**Hotel Santa Bárbara €** *Plaza Santa Bárbara 4-3º, tel: 91-446 2345, www.hostalsantabarbaramadrid.com.* Bargain old-fashioned hostal just outside Chueca, with good Metro links from the airport and around the city.

**Tryp Ambassador €€** *Cuesta Santo Domingo 5–7, tel: 91-541 6700, www.solmelia.com.* This large, handsome hotel on a quiet street near the Palacio Real occupies a magnificent palace and converted monastery, both meticulously renovated. 183 rooms.

## SALAMANCA AND THE PRADO

**Hotel Vincci SoMa €€** *Calle Goya 79, tel: 91-435 7545, www.vinccihoteles.com.* Chic four-star hotel with minimalist decor caters to the very cool crowd. It has a smart fitness suite and a hip restaurant. A classy choice, for Salamanca's upmarket shopping zone. 177 rooms.

**Hotel Mora €** *Paseo del Prado 32, tel: 91-420 1569, www.hotelmora. com.* Down the street from the Prado and the Botanical Garden, this medium-sized (62-roomed) 1930s hotel offers great value for money. Rooms are plain, but they are clean and airy. No groups. Triple rooms available. Busy cafeteria downstairs.

**Hotel Ritz €€€–€€€€** *Plaza de la Lealtad 5, tel: 91-521 1569, www. ritzmadrid.com.* The last word in elegance, this 1910 deluxe hotel is discreetly glamorous and clings to formality (jacket and tie for men). It's extremely expensive and popular with the rich, but non-residents can enjoy afternoon tea in the hall or Sunday brunch on the garden terrace. 167 rooms.

**Hotel Unico €€€** *Claudio Coello 67, tel: 91-7810173, www.unico hotelmadrid.com.* Madrid's newest boutique hotel, both sleek and minimalist, offers personal trainers and shoppers, a lovely patio garden, fitness and wellness suites as well as discreetly luxurious en suite rooms. The restaurant, boasting two Michelin stars, is in the expert hands of Catalan chef Ramón Freixa, and usefully open all day Sunday.

**The Westin Palace €€€–€€€€** *Plaza de las Cortes 7, tel: 91-360 8000, www.westinpalacemadrid.com.* A palatial Belle Epoque hotel opposite Spain's Congress; the five-star, 468-roomed Palace is less formal than the Ritz, but still a chic institution. The hotel combines old-world glamour with a 24-hour business centre and fitness suite. Spectacular glass-roofed domed lounge.

## OUTSIDE MADRID

## ÁVILA

**Parador Raimundo de Borgoña €€** *Marqués de Canales de Chozas 2, tel: 920-211 340, www.parador.es.* Paradores are state-run hotels, usually within renovated historic buildings. This one convincingly updates a 16th-century palace downstairs. Rooms are modern, but homely. Just within Ávila's walls. Good restaurant and summer terrace. 61 rooms.

## SEGOVIA

**Los Linajes €–€€** *Dr Velasco 9, tel: 921-460 475, www.hotelloslinajes. com.* A peaceful, mid-size hotel on a side street in the San Estebán quarter that feels perfectly in sync with old Segovia. Though much of it is a new construction, other parts occupy an 11th-century palace. Some rooms have priceless panoramic views. Restaurant and terrace. 62 rooms.

**Parador de Segovia €–€€** *Carretera de Valladolid s/n, tel: 921-443 737, www.parador.es.* This 1970s state-owned parador has breathtaking views of the magical outline of Segovia, including the Roman aqueduct, medieval walls, cathedral and castle (all illuminated at night). Perched on a hill 3km (2 miles) north of the city, it's less convenient than hotels in the old quarter, but perfect if you've got some time to relax in Segovia. 113 rooms.

## TOLEDO

**Hotel Abad €–€€** *Real del Arrabal 1, tel: 925-283 500, www.hotel abad.com.* This stylishly decorated, three-star independent hotel has 22 rooms, each individually designed. It's set in an old blacksmith's shop; careful renovation has maintained original hand-hewn wooden ceilings. Half price in the low season.

**Hotel Pintor El Greco €–€€** *Calle Alamillos del Tránsito 13, tel: 925-285 191, www.hotelpintorelgreco.com.* This tastefully converted hotel in a 16th-century bakery is in the heart of the old Jewish quarter, next to the El Greco museum and synagogues. The sunny rooms surround a courtyard. Pets allowed. Good views. Breakfast only. 60 rooms.

**Parador Conde de Orgaz €€–€€** *Cerro del Emperador, s/n, tel: 925-221 850, www.parador.es.* This is still the most popular hotel in Madrid for groups. Built as a wooden *ligarrol*, or local farmstead, it has stunning views from the terraces and large swimming pool. Ten minutes' drive from the city. Be sure to reserve in advance. A good choice in summer.

# INDEX

**Berlitz** pocket guide

# Madrid

**Fifth Edition 2013**

Written by Neil Schlecht
Updated by Vicky Hayward
Edited by Carine Tracanelli
Art Editor: Tom Smyth
Series Editor: Tom Stainer
Production: Tynan Dean and Rebeka Ellam

*All Rights Reserved*
© 2013 Apa Publications (UK) Limited

Printed in China by CTPS

Berlitz Trademark Reg. U.S. Patent Office and other countries. Marca Registrada. Used under licence from the Berlitz Investment Corporation

**Photography credits:** Alamy 4BL, 4TR, 51, 93; Bigstock 2/3M, 30, 33; Chris Coe/Apa Publications 19, 87; Corbis 3TR; Dreamstime 2TL, 2TC, 2ML, 4TL, 4/5T, 5TR, 10/11, 28, 29, 38, 42, 55, 60, 62, 65, 66, 74, 83; Esquí España Atudem 97; Glyn Genin/Apa Publications 6ML, 7MC, 40, 54, 64, 67, 78; Gregory Wrona/Apa Publications 4/5M, 5MR; iStockphoto 2MC, 2/3M, 5MC, 7MC, 7TC, 8, 12, 12/13, 15, 24, 26, 31, 32, 34, 37, 39, 41, 52, 53, 56, 58, 71, 73, 77, 81, 84, 92; Jon Santa Cruz/Apa Publications 1, 2/3M, 43, 48, 88, 91, 100, 101, 102, 104, 105; Neal Bucchan-Grant/Apa Publications 6TL, 95; Out of copyright 3TC, 6ML, 17, 23, 44, 45, 47; Scala Archives 3BL, 68; Sipa Press/Rex Features 21; Team Nowitz/Apa Publications 72

**Cover picture:** 4Corners Images

Every effort has been made to provide accurate information in this publication, but changes are inevitable. The publisher cannot be responsible for any resulting loss, inconvenience or injury.

**Contact us**

At Berlitz we strive to keep our guides as accurate and up to date as possible, but if you find anything that has changed, or if you have any suggestions on ways to improve this guide, then we would be delighted to hear from you.

Berlitz Publishing, PO Box 7910,
London SE1 1WE, England.
email: berlitz@apaguide.co.uk
www.insightguides.com/berlitz

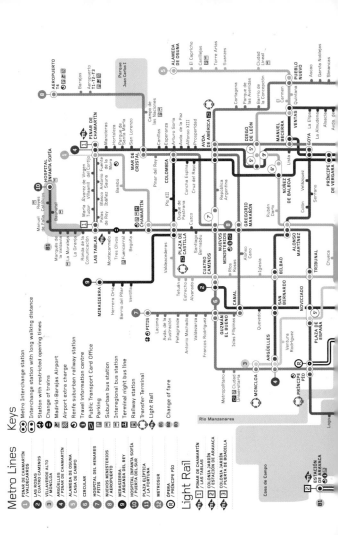

## Metro Lines

- **1** PINAR DE CHAMARTÍN / VALDECARROS
- **2** LAS ROSAS / CUATRO CAMINOS
- **3** VILLAVERDE ALTO / MONCLOA
- **4** ARGÜELLES / PINAR DE CHAMARTÍN
- **5** ALAMEDA DE OSUNA / CASA DE CAMPO
- **6** CIRCULAR
- **7** HOSPITAL DEL HENARES / PITIS
- **8** NUEVOS MINISTERIOS / AEROPUERTO
- **9** MIRASIERRA / ARGANDA DEL REY
- **10** HOSPITAL INFANTA SOFÍA / PUERTA DEL SUR
- **11** PLAZA ELÍPTICA / LA FORTUNA
- **12** METROSUR
- **R** OPERA / PRÍNCIPE PÍO

## Light Rail

- **ML1** PINAR DE CHAMARTÍN / LAS TABLAS
- **ML2** COLONIA JARDÍN / ESTACIÓN DE ARAVACA
- **ML3** COLONIA JARDÍN / PUERTA DE BOADILLA

## Keys

- Metro Interchange station
- Interchange station with long walking distance
- Station with restricted opening times
- Change of trains
- Airport extra charge
- Madrid-Barajas Airport
- Renfe suburban railway station
- Travel information centre
- Public Transport Card Office
- Parking
- Suburban bus station
- Interregional bus station
- Terminal night bus line
- Railway station
- Light Rail
- Transfer Terminal
- Change of fare

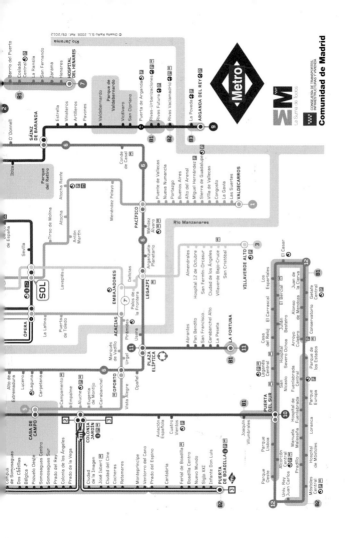

Metro

Comunidad de Madrid
Consorcio de Transportes
Metropolitanos de Madrid

© Diseño RaRo S.L. 2008 Ref. 09/2012

# Berlitz®

speaking your language

**phrase book & dictionary**
**phrase book & CD**

**Available in:** Arabic, Cantonese Chinese, Croatian, Czech, Danish, Dutch, English*, Finnish*, French, German, Greek, Hebrew*, Hindi, Hungarian*, Indonesian, Italian, Japanese, Korean, Latin American Spanish, Mandarin Chinese, Mexican Spanish, Norwegian, Polish, Portuguese, Romanian*, Russian, Spanish, Swedish, Thai, Turkish, Vietnamese

*Book only

www.berlitzpublishing.com